For our daughters

"For the first time in my life, I feel like someone understands the abuse and healing that I have experienced. Now, I have the tools to walk with others down a path of restoration. I have never been able to adequately explain my personal restoration process from victim of sex trafficking to conquerer in Christ. Through *Mending the Soul/Princess Lost,* I have the tools needed to articulate my healing and walk with others to a life of freedom."

—Jessica Richardson, survivor of sex trafficking

"The *Princess Lost/Princess Found* curriculum offers an accessible, beautifully written resource for mentors to walk with survivors of commercial sexual exploitation through the pain of their past into hope for their future. With its engaging illustrations and prose, *Princess Lost* invites the reader to use the story of a young princess to reflect on the inner experience of being lost and thoughtfully consider the joy in being found. The accompanying guide for mentors, *Princess Found,* artfully weaves current research, theory and Scripture in such a way that will prepare mentors to serve survivors with great patience, respect, and love. *Princess Found* continually points us back to our divine mandate: to love in Jesus's name, affirming in each survivor her original design as a beloved daughter of the King."

— Kathy Stout-LaBauve, VP of Aftercare,
International Justice Mission

"Steve and Celestia Tracy bear the beautiful and awful assignment from God to see children and youth trapped in sex trafficking rescued and restored. Facilitating this calling are their years of investment in the theological bedrock of God's heart for such as these, combined with the mental health tools specific to this abuse and trauma. Their background has produced this significant work, truly a gift to those of us who work with so-called throw-away children and youth. Each chapter is essential; each truth is required. And to the church, globally, the next generation of God's people who love the least, last and lost, the Tracys have given an extraordinary foundation upon which to build. Equipped for the work we prayed to do, as we prayed for His Kingdom to come."

—**Kit Danley,** President,
Neighborhood Ministries, Phoenix, Arizona

"From an African culture where storytelling is part of our culture, there is no better way to begin this journey of healing than with a story! *Princess Lost/Princess Found* is very captivating and explains the emotion and behavior of girls and women, who have gone through abuse, in a nonthreatening manner. The pictures perfectly bring out the themes of healing and redemption, and one does not have to have education to understand them. *Princess Lost/Princess Found* prepares caregivers and mentors and helps them count the cost. We have had people coming onboard and wanting to mentor and volunteer in our ministry but they quickly gave up along the way, as they were not able to pay the price of mercy. *Princess Found* is an amazing guidebook! Very profound—giving deep insight into the life of prostituted girls. Through these resources, I have heard the cry and plea of prostituted women, both young and old, commercially and noncommercially exploited, in a way I have never heard before."

—**Marcy Oyoo,** Executive Director,
Full Circle Outreach to Commercial Sex Workers,
Nairobi, Kenya

"The Tracys' unwavering compassion for the abused is matched only by their thorough research. What a gift this is in times like these! *Princess Found* is an invaluable gift to those from whom so much has been taken. I believe its pages will spur hope and healing in many; heaven surely celebrates its release!"

—**Brad Pellish,** Pastor,
Bethany Bible Church, Phoenix, Arizona

"It's hard for me to even try to describe the sense of peace and well-being I have discovered in this process. *Princess Lost* and *Princess Found* have given me a sense of peace and well-being that I have never experienced before. My heart yearns to share this model and my healing with the world. It's going to transform generations."

—**Amira Birger,** survivor of sex trafficking

"It is easy to find a book about sex-trafficking but nearly impossible to find healing curriculum, particularly material that not only explains the effects of sexual abuse and trafficking but offers biblically based steps towards healing. As the founder of a nonprofit organization working with prostituted women in Africa, we have long been asking for material that could be used for counseling and discipling the prostituted women in our programs and now it is finally here! The *Princess Lost/Princess Found* curricula is precisely what we have needed. Scripture, research, and real-life examples are beautifully integrated and arranged into a clear pathway, equipping caregivers and counselors in supporting the healing of prostituted girls. I highly recommend these works for anyone who wants to understand the dynamics of sex trafficking and desires to reach out and help victims heal."

—**Abigail Tracy Kakeeto,** Founder and Director
of A Perfect Injustice, Kampala, Uganda

"Sex-trafficking has increased greatly in the last two decades because of the collapse of communism, globalization, and the fear of AIDS. Over 100 million girls are missing from the globe today. Steve and Celestia Tracy have provided part of the solution: a reliable, tested, and informative guide for mentors of sexually exploited girls, including interactive exercises, music, and art. They go beyond psychological and sociological frames, providing a biblically sound and theologically rich reading of alienation, shame, and redemption."

—**John DelHousaye,** Associate Professor of
New Testament, Phoenix Seminary

"By weaving a masterful tale of redemption in the face of appalling evil and cruelty, Steve and Celestia Tracy provide hope for all the 'daughters of our city,' based upon the truth of Scripture and the only Hope—Jesus Christ."

—**Paul Madson,** Founder and President,
Global Training Network

"I have worked with abused children as adult survivors of childhood abuse. With little success, I have looked for tools that would help facilitate healing to those places in a child's heart that have been so deeply wounded. The PL & PF curriculum does this like no other resource I have ever seen. Children of all ages and cultures embrace the beauty of art, music, and story contained in this curriculum, to touch areas which are often impenetrable in the heart of a survivor. This curriculum provides those who work alongside victims of abuse a glimpse into their world, which is something that survivors so desperately long for. Whether you are a professional with years of education and experience or the friend or loved one of someone who has been through the ravaging effects of abuse, you will gain a newfound depth of insight and understanding into the far-reaching effects of childhood sexual abuse."

—**Samia Kamel-Ohm MA, LPC, NCC,** Licensed Professional Counselor, Hope Restores Counseling

"*Princess Found* is both an expressive and practical guide for the compassionate caregivers who desire to lead others into relational, emotional, and spiritual healing. The Tracys' emphasis on the importance of healing within the context of relationships, combined with a clear discussion of current research and relevant use of Scripture, allow *Princess Lost* and *Princess Found* to be incredible resources for those desiring to walk alongside of sexually exploited girls in their process of healing."

—**Kim Chaves,** MA, LPC, Christian counselor in private practice

"The Tracys have taken dark and evil topics and provided both abuse survivors and their mentors the tools to bring their stories into the light and presence of God's grace. *Princess Lost* is a well-written story with beautiful pictures and graphics—readers will want to linger on each and every page. *Princess Found* equips us to journey into the depths of this complicated subject—providing valuable insights and discussion topics. The two books together are absolutely brilliant!"

—**Jody Ann Noon, RN, JD,** Administrator, Office of Community Health & Health Planning, Oregon State Health Division

"Running through *Princess Found* and *Princess Lost* is the mission and insight of Steven and Celestia Tracy for the sexual exploitation and trafficking of women. The combination of the fairy tale (*Princess Lost*) and the Mentor's Guide (*Princess Found*) anticipates both the needs of the exploited and the training of the advocate. While the social science brings vital explanation, I was especially struck by the quality of theological insight that adds prophetic urgency and enables pastoral care. Here is no fairy tale, but the archetypal story of plundered women. The 'Interactive Exercises' closing out each chapter are practical and downright therapeutic. Social worker, pastor, and therapist now have a balanced and integrative tool—thanks for removing our excuses!"

—**Andrew J. Schmutzer, PhD,** Professor of Biblical Studies, Moody Bible Institute, author of *The Long Journey Home: Understanding and Ministering to the Sexually Abused*

"Many have answered the call to help these girls yet were without the tools necessary to care for them amidst the complexities of the aftermath left in their souls by what they have endured. *Princess Lost* and *Princess Found* give us the foundation and understanding we need to ensure every church is a safe church and every leader a safe leader for 'our girls.'"

—**Tammy J. Smith,** Pastor of Spiritual Formation, Paradise Valley Community Church

"As I pondered the words to express how MTS/PL has changed my life, I was flooded with too much to say. I was first of all tremendously honored to be a part of something so instrumental to outreach to sexually exploited youth and grateful for how this curriculum has UN-distorted my life. I have such a unique and undeniable story, that I feel overwhelmed with relief and appreciation for the peace, strength, and wisdom that have been given to me by the grace of GOD through these resources. I have always known Jesus as my Savior, but as I've learned, my view of him was unwillingly distorted by evil, trauma, and shame. *Princess Lost/Princess Found* has helped me realize the truth that God was with me during my abuse. It has also helped me understand physically, psychologically, emotionally, but most of all, spiritually what was going on inside of me and what I was feeling for so long. *Princess Lost/Princess Found* has been my long prayed for answer to a gaping wound that I buried deep in my soul. Mending the Soul has truly become my anchor to the truth and my bridge to redemption! I know now what is real and I understand how to use my sorrow to help others, which has been for me, the only way to fully heal. You have inspired strength in me that I never knew I could have. One voice is all it takes! I will return to the darkness, strong, fearless, with my mended soul ready to speak the truth and save other precious lives from this invisible hell on earth."

—**Kay,** survivor of sex trafficking

"*Princess Lost/Princess Found* are the best resources we have found to help our caregivers and mentors understand the sexually exploited girls and to know how to help them heal. The Mending the Soul model embedded in *Princess Found* creates the safety, support, and freedom for the sexually exploited girls of our ministry. As caregivers, when we need equipping and support, we can go to PL/PF for resources and direction that guide the healing of our girls. There is no other resource like it!"

—**Fran Gonzales,** Executive Director,
The Rescue Project, Phoenix, Arizona

PRINCESS FOUND

A Guide for Mentors of Sexually Exploited Girls

MENDING
THE SOUL
BRINGING HOPE TO GENERATIONS

STEVEN R. TRACY AND CELESTIA G. TRACY

Princess Found
Library of Congress Control Number: 2011935912
ISBN 9780981968582
ISBN categories - social science/spirituality

Contents

Acknowledgments

Without our beautiful daughters who have entrusted us with their stories, this book would not have been written. We think especially of Amira Birger, whom God brought first to Mending the Soul (MTS) for healing, and now is one of our most fearless and passionate mentors—telling her story over and over again for the restoration of many.

Thank you, Kayla Tracy, our daughter in love. You said "yes" when asked to create 36 separate pieces of original art for *Princess Lost*. Your vision gave pictures to the complexities of abuse, healing, and redemption. Thank you, musicians David and Ree Boado, Noel Barto, Amber Hunter, Justan Jesse, Toby Milford and Gregory Naylor, for recording the songs, background music, and audio of *Princess Lost*. You created, composed, and sang from honest and raw hearts, giving freely to sisters and daughters you may never meet. You created with a fury of passion and vision, inspired by the Spirit who was fitting the art, to the story, to the song.

Thank you, Dan Brenner and McMurry. You consistently supported the creation and production of these healing resources, leveraging in as guardian over the inception and design. Thank you, Lisa Altomare, for lovingly and patiently crafting print-ready files out of our storyboard and original art. Thank you to our editors, David Creech, John Dickerson, Deb Beatty, Beth Tomkiw and Cindy Hutchinson. Your insight and skill have enhanced these resources and prepared them for publication.

Thank you, Dagny Mallory, our director of operations at

Mending the Soul Ministries. Your watchful care over each detail kept us focused and moving forward, and then, as your ultimate gift, you gave your own story of bondage and redemption so that others might give voice to their own.

Thank you, Peggy Bilsten. As Vice Mayor of Phoenix, you shined the light on child prostitution and tirelessly advocated for the lost princesses of our city. You did it alone, until others found their way to this issue and joined you in this worthy work.

Thank you to the many leaders who sacrificially gave of themselves so that this book would become a reality and be offered as a gift to the many caregivers and girls in need of care. Thank you, filmmaker Brittany Lefebvre, for your vision, leadership, and partnership with MTS and our *Princess* project. Your team—Diego, Luisa, and Philip—has been invaluable to these resources and MTS.

Thank you to the pastors who gave us our start, Pastor Lee McFarland of Radiant Church and Pastor Brad Pellish of Bethany Bible Church. You provided financial support and an office in the heart of our city, when this book and these resources were just a vision and not yet a reality. Thank you for believing in us, and the MTS community, and for investing in this work. Thank you, Streetlight Phoenix, for requesting faith-based healing resources for the girls of your shelter and beyond.

Thank you, community leaders of faith, for supporting *Princess Lost* and hosting training and benefit concerts for your communities: Pastor Tammy Smith of Paradise Valley Community Church, Poiema, Door to Grace, ASU Campus Crusade, Without Walls, Whitton Avenue Bible Church, and Antioch Church of God in Christ. For Suzi Kaminsky, and your T-shirt/necklace design, for Andi Pearson, Brian Fergus, and Katie Resendiz from The International Rescue Committee, for painstakingly writing grants. For the many who gave sacrificially for the daughters they may never meet: Ryan and Linda Bale, Tim and Elizabeth Boyd, Joe and Jenny Brackman, Tomi Clark, Darryl and Holly DelHousaye, Mary Dietrich, Marvin and Cinda Feidler, Jim and Tanya Harris, Mark and Linda Hoyt, Jody and Jeanie Humber, Gary and Diane Lauterbach, Brittany Lefebvre, Shawn and Dagny Mallory (and friends), Janet Martin, Janice Parks, Nora Poling, David and Kimberly Standfast, Christine Stephenson, Steve and Celestia Tracy, Gary and Helen Williams, Damascus Road Tucson, Paradise Valley Community Church, Sundt Foundation, and Without Walls Christian Center. Thank you to Mending the Soul Ministries for making these *Princess Lost* resources a reality: Dagny Mallory, Peggy Bilsten, Peter Kinkel, Roxane Thorstad, Jon Brecke, Jim and Tanya Harris, Nora Poling, Kent and Blanca Bertrand, and Janet Martin. Thank you to the hundreds of MTS facilitators, clinicians, and our *Princess Lost* mentors, who boldly went first in our city, offering healing and care to those who were desperate for support. You charged the darkness and found Christ there. Thank you for boldly using your stories to create safety and healing for others.

And finally, my warmest thanks to Steven, my soul mate for thirty-two years. Without your research and expertise in the formation of this manuscript, it would not have its framework and foundation. To our precious children—Tim, Elizabeth, Luke, and Kayla, our U.S. partners, and David and Abigail, our African partners, who have taught us so much, while serving the poorest of the poor in Kampala, Uganda. I cannot write your names without tears in my eyes.

Our greatest praise and gratitude go to our Lord and Savior, Jesus Christ, who calls us to partner with him in this joy-filled work; who went first with the ultimate sacrifice of His life so that we might know we are truly His beloved.

foreword

*My eyes overflow with rivers of water for the
destruction of the daughters of my people.
My eyes flow and do not cease, without
interruption, till the Lord from heaven looks
down and sees. My eyes bring suffering to my
soul because of all the daughters of my city.*
LAMENTATIONS 3:48–51 (NKJV)

Our hearts have been inalterably broken over the epidemic
of slavery experienced both domestically and globally today.
It is inconceivable to many of us that these atrocities are being
perpetrated in our cities and communities. After gathering and synthesizing much of the social science research,
we found surprisingly few resources to guide the Christian
leaders who desire to support exploited adolescent girls in
their cities. As we became increasingly aware of the need for
resources, we knew it was our responsibility to do *something*.
This is that something—a collective project that we humbly
offer to the great hearts who are already in the trenches of
this dark epidemic, loving exploited children with the love of
Christ. This book is for you.

I work with trauma survivors every day and have done so
since 1993. As a result, I have spent most of my professional
life listening, and I have been profoundly impacted by what
I have heard. My husband, Steven, is a seminary professor,
theologian, and ethicist who has dedicated much of his

professional life to researching, writing, and teaching on issues of abuse/trauma and sexual ethics. In 2003, we founded Mending the Soul (MTS) Ministries and currently work with a multidisciplinary team to equip communities of faith with the research, resources, and training necessary to provide an informed and compassionate response to abuse survivors. We consider ourselves students who continue to listen and learn from the survivors who entrust us with their stories.

In 2005, Zondervan published *Mending the Soul: Understanding and Healing Abuse*. The underlying theology of abuse and healing in this *Guide for Mentors of Sexually Exploited Girls* is further expanded in that book. *Princess Lost* and *Princess Found* are thus built on the foundation of *Mending the Soul*. Together, *Princess Lost* and *Princess Found* narrow the focus of abuse healing to a specific group of survivors—sexually exploited girls and women.

The Mending the Soul model is premised on the robust belief that the most effective and potent "helper" for an abused person is another who has experienced similar abuse and subsequent healing. MTS employs a community-based model of care that equips survivors with resources and training, empowering them to use their story to support others just beginning their healing journey. In this mentoring relationship, both participants continue to move toward restoration and wholeness.

Abuse happens in relationships, therefore healing must happen in relationships. The treatment of trauma must not be confined to a professional, medical, or psychological response, but instead understood as a relational process. *A community-based model of care understands healing not as the domain solely belonging to a handful of experts, but as a holistic, community task in which numerous individuals, within the context of various healthy, relational communities, utilize their unique skills and gifts to facilitate restoration.* We have seen this community-based model work, both domestically and globally.

There is surprisingly little research on sexually exploited female minors. As a result, there is much that we do not know about them. However, to offer the best possible care for survivors of exploitation, we need both a solid understanding of the existing social science research and a robust theology of abuse and healing. *Princess Found: A Guide for Mentors of Sexually Exploited Girls* is not a complete treatise on the sexual exploitation of female minors. Instead, this book serves as a tool to help one begin to understand sexual exploitation, its effects, and the healing relationship. This resource is not intended to take the place of professional counseling or other mental health services, but instead to supplement those services as a user-friendly tool for the community-based, holistic mentoring of exploited girls. May these resources serve as a gentle guide in the unfolding of a survivor's story: both her royal origins as God's creation and the ways in which she has been betrayed and exploited.

> *My people are destroyed for lack of knowledge.*
> HOSEA 3:6

Research tells us that most sexually exploited adolescents have been sexually abused early in life, and this early trauma has significantly impacted their neurological development. Traumatic memories are stored in the brain differently than other memories and, therefore, lack "verbal narrative and context; rather, they are encoded in the form of vivid sensations and images."[1] These sensations are intrusive and frightening for the survivor and are often difficult to access through conversation. The child's fears and behaviors are specifically related to the traumatic events they have experienced. Yet their trauma has been stored in a part of the brain where it is unavailable for normal recall or cognitive processing.

Princess Lost is a fairy tale that gently mirrors many elements of a traumatized girl's story of sexual exploitation. Reading this story will help her begin to understand and integrate extremely painful realities about her traumatic experiences in a sensitive way. *Princess Lost* empowers her to "direct" her own healing—as she is encouraged to attend to the images, words, and metaphors that move her. *Princess Lost* simplifies the complexities of the evil she has experienced, fitting them into a more manageable framework. *Princess Lost* gives young survivors an opportunity to reach back into a childhood that was brutally snatched away. The story puts each survivor in touch with a world that she knows exists, but has *never existed for her.* The survivor is offered a glimpse into a childhood and innocence that was lost as well as a vision of her life redeemed. We do not know of a better or more visceral way of describing God's supernatural good triumphing over evil than through this genre. Realistic descriptions fail us in this endeavor.[2]

> I now enjoy the fairy tales better than I did in childhood: being now able to put more in, of course, I get more out.[3]
> —C. S. LEWIS

The twelve chapters of *Princess Found: A Guide for Mentors of Sexually Exploited Girls* correspond to the twelve chapters in *Princess Lost* and explain the social science research as well as the Scripture that caregivers need to support their survivors. This book is designed to give the reader an accurate and detailed understanding of the experiences and unique needs of sexually exploited girls and to offer practical suggestions for the use of the fairy tale itself. In each chapter, we include suggestions for interactive exercises as appropriate for the girl and her setting. We have also created the *Princess Lost Journal* to prompt and direct the intrapersonal, emotionally connecting exercises that coordinate with *Princess Lost* and *Princess Found: A Guide for Mentors. Princess Lost* includes a healing music CD that corresponds to its twelve chapters. The use of music furthers the multisensory experience for traumatized girls and thus facilitates emotional expression and healing.[4]

Prostituted minors suffer some of the most severe and complex physical, emotional, and spiritual damage of any wounded population. As such, pastors, volunteers, and staff must have the necessary education and training to understand these girls' unique issues and needs. This understanding is essential to knowing them and, through knowing them, helping them heal. A theology of God's love and mercy shows us the way.

You will likely encounter spiritual warfare as you join God in working to "set captives free." When you do sense discouragement or spiritual conflict, revisit the steps of self-care suggested at the end of chapter eleven. Also, before you get started, prayerfully read the four appendices found at the end of this guide: Mentor Safety, Mentor Readiness, Self-Screen Questionnaire for Mentors, and Feeling Charts.

Thank you for reading this book and for dedicating yourself to this costly, sacred, and life-changing service. May these resources encourage and support you as you reach out to this most wounded and often invisible population of girls. We have written *Princess Found* for men and women who are not mere bystanders but dedicated, committed participants in the battle against sexual exploitation. We assume that you are serving or will serve specific girls, each with a unique name, gifts, and history. We assume that you do not view exploited girls as mere tragic statistics to acknowledge or "needy projects" to pity but as daughters to lovingly serve. Thus, we will repeatedly refer to "your girls" in this guide— the girls for whom you have taken personal responsibility, with God's help, to learn to walk beside and assist.

> *Now faith is being sure of what we hope for*
> *and certain of what we do not see.*
> *Who through faith, conquered kingdoms,*
> *administered justice,*
> *and gained what was promised;*
> *who shut the mouths of lions;*
> *Quenched the fury of the flames,*
> *and escaped the edge of the sword;*
> ***Whose weakness was turned to strength;***
> *And who became powerful in battle*
> *and routed foreign armies ...*
> *Therefore, since we are surrounded by such a*
> *great cloud of witnesses,*
> *Let us throw off everything that hinders and the*
> *sin that so easily entangles,*
> *And let us run with perseverance the race*
> *marked out for us.*
> *Let us fix our eyes on Jesus,*
> *the author and perfecter of our faith,*
> *Who for the joy set before him endured the cross,*
> *Scorning its shame,*
> *And sat down at the right hand of*
> *the throne of God. ...*

Therefore, strengthen your feeble arms
and weak knees.
Make level paths for your feet,
So that the lame may not be disabled,
but rather healed.
HEBREWS 11:1, 33–35A; 12:1–2A, 12–13

Introduction

That the living may know that the Most High
rules in the kingdom of men.
You are able, for the Spirit of the Holy God
is in you.
DANIEL 4:17–18 (NKJV)

God has called our daughter Abby to serve him among the street children of Kampala, Uganda. The following quote from her blog[5] demonstrates both the difficulty and the reward of ministering to survivors of abuse:

> I realized something the other day. The longer I live in Uganda, the more evil and beauty I see in the world, the more I see the loving hand of God in everything and am drawn to Him. ... It is so strange. Yesterday was really a very normal day in the life of a slum in downtown Kampala, Uganda. I walked into the Kivulu slum this morning to a large crowd shouting and cheering on police officers as they beat baayai—bad people—out of the area. They hadn't stolen anything ... yet. I met a new street boy who had been living on the streets with his mother, who had lost her mind and had just recently died, leaving him on the streets alone. That night, I brought cups of hot tea and said good night to over fifty children sleeping in their burlap sacks in the dirt with their little street dogs curled around them. I took away

drugs from a very high nine-year-old boy who was sway-
ing shirtless with glazed eyes telling me that he didn't
have anything. I passed a woman bartering with a man
in a grimy dark alleyway over the price for which she
was willing to sell her body. I watched more baayai by
the entrance of our house roll up joints as my kids [the
unofficially adopted street children whom I care for] ignored them and helped us carry the heavy beds inside.

Life in Uganda is not perfect and for many street kids
very difficult. But I wouldn't trade it for anything. I have
found that it is through that darkness that the most
beautiful redemption, grace, and brightness emerge.
Here you have to ask for miracles every day, and the
beautiful thing is, God performs them."[6]

Words cannot express our gratitude to God for the transformational work he is doing in Abby's life. By God's grace, I
have gained deeper insights into the doctrines of humanity,
sin, and redemption through her ministry than through most
of my formal studies in theology and Bible, including a PhD
in New Testament ethics. Multiple conferences in the Democratic Republic of the Congo, supporting trauma survivors
and outreach to sexually exploited and trafficked youth in the
United States and eastern Africa, have added to these lessons
and transformed us. Our real-world understanding and application of biblical truth has been deepened.

It is one thing, while enjoying a comfortable life in a rela-
tively secure American suburb, to affirm verbally, "God so
loved the world," "Every human being is made in God's image
and has worth and value," "The cross of Christ has the power
to transform needy sinners," and "God answers prayer." It

is another matter altogether to live out these truths in the midst of darkness, as our hearts break over the evil and misery we have witnessed. As we shudder over human sin. And when every conceivable human resource is unable to heal or change vast and destructive circumstances.

Like our daughter, we have discovered that it is through darkness "that the most beautiful redemption, grace, and brightness emerge. Here you have to ask for miracles every day, and the beautiful thing is, God performs them." We don't have to live in an African slum to experience these precious truths. They apply to us whenever we care in Jesus's name for the sexually exploited, whether they find themselves in the child brothels of India, the slums of Kampala, or the suburbs of Phoenix.

Sound biblical, theological understanding is essential for spiritual growth and effective Christian service. Scripture is God's powerful, living, life-transforming word (Heb 4:12). God is the Supreme Creator of the universe, so all of life, including sexual exploitation—especially sexual exploitation—can only be understood properly through the lens of Scripture. Thus, this *Guide for Mentors* is grounded in a biblical and theological understanding of sexual exploitation and healing.

It is essential at the beginning of this book to remind the reader that, in the midst of the daunting challenge of outreach to survivors of sexual exploitation, Scripture must be our guide, solace, and sustenance. Sexual exploitation is one of the most destructive, evil, and painful realities we will ever confront. None of us possesses the innate power, wisdom, or resilience for this work. These come only from Christ. We will only grow in intimacy and knowledge of Christ as we feed on his word, hearing and humbly submitting to his voice, letting his truth mold and direct all we are and do.

Before we proceed further we should clarify some of the
critical terms relevant to sexual abuse and exploitation, particularly involving minors. We will define four closely related
terms. In doing so, it is important to understand that each
of these activities encompasses a broad continuum of behaviors, all of which are morally wrong and very destructive.

Commercial sexual exploitation. A National Institute of Justice
Special Report states: *"The commercial sexual exploitation of children
(CSEC) is sexual abuse of a minor for economic gain. It involves physical abuse, pornography, prostitution, and the smuggling of children for
unlawful purposes."*[7]

Commercial sex trafficking: The federal Trafficking Victims
Protection Act of 2000 (TVPA) defines commercial sex trafficking as a "severe" form of human trafficking involving: *(A)
a commercial sex act [which] is induced by force, fraud, or coercion,
or in which the person induced to perform such act has not attained
18 years of age; or (B) the recruitment, harboring, transportation,
provision, or obtaining of a person for labor or services, through the
use of force, fraud, or coercion for the purpose of subjection to invol-
untary servitude.*[8] *Several things are critical in defining commercial
sex trafficking:*

1. It involves the exchange of something of value—money,
   drugs, shelter, etc., for a sex act. Thus, it is "commercial."

2. It involves force, fraud, or coercion if the one being exploited is an adult (18 years of age or older).

3. It only needs to involve a commercial exchange for a
   sex act if the one committing the sex act is a minor.

Thus, by definition, minors can be commercially sex trafficked even if force, fraud, or coercion is not used. Furthermore, based on federal legislation, commercial sex trafficking does not technically need to involve transport across state lines or even proof of the physical movement of a victim.[9]

Thus, commercial sexual exploitation and commercial sex trafficking as defined here are very closely related terms *that describe some form of sexual abuse in which a sex act is exchanged for something of value.* Since commercial sexual exploitation has a more intuitive meaning and is less technical, it is the term we will prefer in *Princess Found.* It will encompass "commercial sex trafficking."

Sexual abuse. Commercial sexual exploitation and sexual abuse are similar—both involve destructive sexual exploitation and both are criminal. Sexual abuse, however, does not involve a commercial transaction. By definition, *child sexual abuse is the exploitation of a minor for the sexual gratification of another person through sexual contact or sexual interaction.*[10] Abusive sexual contact encompasses a wide spectrum of increasingly intrusive types of contact, from sexual kissing to touching clothed breasts or clothed pubic area to touching/fondling breasts, to touching/fondling genitals, to oral sex, to intercourse. Abusive sexual interaction involves such acts as deliberate exposure of a minor to pornography, sexual acts, or one's own sexual organs (exhibitionism). *Adult sexual abuse is "any sexual act in which the woman or man does not consent."*[11] This is often referred to as "rape." It is important to recognize that consent is irrelevant to the act of child abuse. This is based on the fact that sexual relations between an adult and a minor cannot truly involve objective, reasonable consent on the part of the minor because: (1) minors do not have fully developed cognitive and emotional faculties; (2) there is an inherent (and unfair) power imbalance between adults and minors.

Noncriminal sexual exploitation: "Sexual exploitation" is often used in a technical legal sense. But "exploitation" is also used by sociologists to describe a relationship in which one person is mistreated or "used" for the benefit of others. Thus, *noncriminal sexual exploitation occurs when an adult mistreats another adult by using them sexually for their own unfair benefit.* This normally involves manipulation based on a person's relational, emotional, or economic vulnerability. For instance, it is surprisingly common for middle-aged professionals to "date" very young women, give them expensive gifts, and even offer them a free apartment in which to live. It is tacitly expected that the girl, who may well be 18 years old, unemployed, frightfully naive, and very desperate, will be available sexually to this man whenever he is in town or whenever he wants to go out on a "date." In this type of social arrangement the man is often called a "sugar daddy." There are many other ways that vulnerable young women (or men) are manipulated and sexually exploited even though the behavior may not meet the legal definition of a crime. Caregivers must be sensitive to the reality and dynamics of noncriminal sexual exploitation, for it is very common and is often every bit as emotionally and spiritually destructive as criminal sexual exploitation. In some respects it may be more destructive because it is extremely difficult for the victim to recognize that he or she had been harmfully victimized if the behavior was not technically illegal.

Survivors as Image Bearers of God

We would now like to introduce briefly some foundational biblical teaching on the doctrine of humanity, which will be woven
throughout this book. This theology drives the themes of *Princess Lost*. Some may wonder why we use a "princess lost" motif.

Should we really view people in general, and the sex trafficked
in particular, as lost princes and princesses? Is this a biblical
way of viewing the world? After all, in much of contempo-
rary Western culture, it seems our problem is that we think
too highly of ourselves. Influential New Age writers speak of
"finding the goddess within." Secular self-help writers and
entertainers make fortunes telling us that we are great, that
we must believe in ourselves, and that we can do anything we
think we can. While such secular views of human nature are
unbiblical, we must not seek to correct them by overreacting
and minimizing biblical truth about human value and dignity. We do well to ask ourselves whether most people really see
themselves as God sees them—as "fearfully and wonderfully
made" by the Lord of the universe (Ps 139:14). Do victims
of abuse and exploitation know that the King values them
so much that he paid the ultimate price to have a personal
relationship with them? Do they know that He crafted them
as an individual, in his very image?

"Image of God" is the most foundational and defining
characteristic of human beings. In the creation account of
Genesis 1:1–2:25, humanity is described as the pinnacle of
creation, for only man and woman are made in the image
and likeness of God. This is what distinguishes us from animals and everything else in the universe. Only we humans
are made like God, uniquely reflecting his attributes. And
thus, only we have unique, inestimable, and eternal value

and worth. This remains true, even in a fallen world where people often do not appear very God-like.

Psalm 8 proclaims this truth in dramatic fashion, beginning and ending with a bold declaration of God's majesty: "O Lord, our Lord, how majestic is your name in all the earth!" After affirming the glory of God reflected in the universe, the psalmist asks a most logical question regarding people: "When I look at your heavens, the work of your fingers, the moon and the stars that you have established; what are human beings that you are mindful of them, mortals that you care for them?" (Pss 8:3–4, NRSV).

In other words, in view of the greatness of the universe, is it even reasonable to assume that finite and sinful human beings are "any more than a rash on the epidermis of the earth?"[12] The psalmist immediately gives a shocking answer to his own question regarding human identity and significance: "Yet you have made them a little lower than God, and crowned them with glory and honor" (Ps 8:5, NRSV). What a staggering assessment of the human race! In spite of the fact that we are flawed, frail, and sinful, God has invested us with intrinsic majesty and dignity, making us a little lower than God himself.[13] We are truly the princes and princesses of the King of the universe!

In a very real sense, the mission of God is a *Princess Lost* story, a story in which God redeems the fallen and flawed people who were made in his very image. The last thing Satan wants anyone to embrace is that he or she is a prince or princess, made and loved by God Almighty. Satan strategically destroys by deceiving people into defining themselves by the twisted messages they hear from others. This is particularly true for sexually exploited youth, who come to believe they are what verbally malicious parents, sexual abusers, insecure peers, pimps, rap singers, johns, and pornographers have, in words and actions, told them they are: ugly losers, pieces of meat good only for men's lustful pleasure, dirty sluts who deserve to be beaten and raped, stupid little bitches who will never be able to do anything but sell their bodies to anyone with a few grimy dollar bills, disgusting whores God can't wait to destroy.

Because of these satanic lies, it is essential that we caregivers hold to a robustly biblical view of humanity, allowing God's truth to shape our minds and open our eyes, so that we come to view every person we meet the way He views them. This is particularly important with survivors of sexual exploitation. Each survivor is a majestic creation of God with a specific purpose, a beautiful design and an eternal destiny.

Our privilege and calling is, with God's strength, to help lost princesses and princes find their way back to their Creator, their Papa King, so that they can enjoy a love relationship with him for all eternity. C.S. Lewis brilliantly describes these truths as follows:

> It is a serious thing to live in a society of possible gods and goddesses, to remember that the dullest and most uninteresting person you talk to may one day be a creature which, if you saw it now, you would be strongly tempted to worship, or else a horror and a corruption such as you now meet, if at all, only in a nightmare. All day long we are, in some degree, helping each other to one or other of these destinations. … There are no "ordinary" people. You have never talked to a mere mortal. Nations, cultures, arts, civilizations—these are mortal, and their life is to ours as the life of a gnat. But it is

immortals whom we joke with, work with, marry, snub, and exploit—immortal horrors or
everlasting splendours. [Thus, from the outset,
we must take] each other seriously—no flip-
pancy, no superiority, no presumption. And
our charity must be a real and costly love.[14]

Every sexually exploited girl, as well as every pimp and john
we will ever meet, is immortal. Not one of them is an "ordinary
person." They are in need of finding their way home. This redemptive mission will require our most real and costly love.[14]

Courageous Listening

"No one ever listens." These words are often the first words
spoken within minutes of meeting a survivor of childhood
sexual exploitation. Whatever else they may be saying to us,
they are beseeching us: "Listen to me. Please listen." Their
very lives depend on that listening. When any of us speaks,
we expect to be heard. Sadly when we speak and we're not
heard, we have increasingly less to say, and, therefore, less
to ask for. Eventually, we may stop talking altogether as the
"lights of our being steadily darken."[15] One of the hideous
tragedies of early childhood exploitation is the loss of self
due to the lack of relational safety and nurturing presence.
As caregivers, our greatest and most challenging task is to
create physical, emotional, and psychological safety for the
reactivation of the spirit of the survivor.

Jennifer Freyd develops the concept of *courageous listening*
versus *active listening* as a necessary component in a healing
relationship. She states:

> Stories of trauma, by necessity, begin in frag-
> mented and sometimes implausible ways.
> They evoke strong reactions in listeners, from
> compassion to outright rejection. They scare
> us, they anger us, and they never leave us
> untouched. It is easy to distance ourselves or
> become vicariously traumatized by them. There-
> fore, it is tempting to settle for a technique of
> "active listening" … which sacrifices emotional
> depth and truth for surface particulars. It is
> harder to hold on to the uncertainty necessary
> as an individual struggles for the emotional
> truth embedded in traumatic events.[16]

Our challenge is to allow our expectations and thinking to be altered and changed by what we hear. This process is known as mutuality: "affecting the other and being affected by the other; one extends oneself out to another and is also receptive to the impact of the other. There is openness to influence, emotional availability, and a constantly changing pattern of responding to and affecting the other's state. There is both receptivity and active initiative toward the other."[17]

How do we do this? By listening to and believing in the story as it is given—without doubting, rejecting, or expressing shock, listening with the desire of "experiencing" it with her, as if we were her, so that she does not have to re-experience it alone. This kind of listening is costly and will require a great deal from us. This kind of listening heals because it literally lifts and imports the pain of another into oneself. This is the very action Christ takes with us—Immanuel: *God with us.* He joins us in our pain. He is there in our deepest place of suffering.

As we listen courageously to others, they are helped to find a voice that they have never used before. They are awakened to parts of themselves that they have never experienced before. As we listen, survivors will find more confident voices and begin to trust that they will be heard. This is a sacred process that allows for the discovery of the originally designed self.[18]

Transformed by Pain

Courageous listening is foundational in creating safe and healthy environments where trauma survivors can heal. The "right person" for this therapeutic relationship is someone who has sat in the shadows and pain of his or her own life long enough to find Christ's healing presence there. It is in our own healing that we will experience, sometimes for the first time, the intimate presence of Christ which pours over our shamed, exposed, and aching hearts. Many of us have stories of experiencing Christ's love first through the gentle touch of a safe, nurturing human being, and then through the anointing, loving presence of Christ *in our pain.*

Ironically, for many of us, our spiritual traditions have taught us to run from and deny our painful past in order to be accepted and belong. We've been fooled into thinking that God expects us to be always happy and have pain-free lives in this age. We may also be tempted to believe that we can somehow reach into the ache of this world without getting dirty, that we can be the hands of Christ while maintaining pain-free lives. However, this is not true. Instead, God is asking us to move into the darkness around us, to trade our pain for Christ's presence, in order to offer ongoing restoration to others.

We rarely think of pain as something that comes from God's loving providence, as a valuable resource to be used for him. Yet this is what Scripture teaches.[19] God does not want us to deny our pain. Neither does he want us to hide or wallow in our pain. Instead, He wants to use our pain for our good and the good of others.

For instance, the Apostle Paul suffered a chronic "thorn in the flesh"—some sort of physical or material pain sent by Satan (2 Cor 12:7–10). Paul pleaded with God to remove his painful "thorn." While this was an appropriate prayer, and God does heal some pain in this life, God did not choose to heal Paul. And for us, sometimes he does not immediately heal. In fact, even the healings God gives us now are incomplete. Total healing will happen when we stand in God's presence and all pain is removed forever (Rev 21:3–4). Until that day, we look to God in the midst of our pain, allowing pain to work as a powerful redemptive tool. God's response to Paul's request is very instructive. God lovingly replied, "[No, I won't heal you because] my grace is sufficient for you, for my power is made perfect in weakness" (2 Cor 12:9). God asked Paul to trust him and to entrust his pain to him. It was Paul's human weakness reflected in chronic pain that forced him to rely on Christ and experience more of his power. That pain allowed God's power to flow through Paul's weakness to others who were weak, in pain, and in need of the healing power that only comes from God. Earlier in the epistle, Paul elaborates on this truth: As we experience comfort from God in the midst of our pain, we are able to share his comfort with others in pain.

Praise be to the God and Father of our Lord
Jesus Christ, the Father of compassion and

*the God of all comfort, who comforts us in all
our troubles, so that we can comfort those in
any trouble with the comfort we ourselves have
received from God. For just as the sufferings
of Christ flow over into our lives, so also
through Christ our comfort overflows. If we are
distressed, it is for your comfort and salvation;
if we are comforted, it is for your comfort,
which produces in you patient endurance of the
same sufferings we suffer.*
2 CORINTHIANS 1:3–6 NIV

As caregivers, we must note that the pain Paul describes in this passage is a narrower kind of pain; namely, the pain that results from sacrificially serving others. Being Jesus's hands and feet to a broken world, extending his love to those in need, is costly. For example, those who want to effectively minister to street children in Africa must be willing to face a host of risks, sacrifices, and pains, from tropical diseases to loneliness, physical assaults, and burdensome life-and-death responsibilities in the care of others. Paul understood well these specific ministry costs (2 Cor 11:7–32). Similarly, as we minister to prostituted girls, we experience much pain. What we see and hear haunts us. If we have trauma in our past, it will likely resurface during our ministry to a survivor. We may be physically threatened by pimps, johns, and even by prostituted girls. This ministry is financially costly and may bring material pain. In this sense, we will experience Christ-likeness, voluntarily moving ourselves into the pain of others.

In addition to joining in the suffering of Christ himself, we also accelerate God's comfort and grace in our own life, as we minister to survivors. Paul gives us a counterintuitive but essential spiritual principle—the more pain we experience (pain that is a necessary part of serving others), the more we experience God's comfort, and the more we are able to give God's comfort to others. This illustrates a powerful pain/joy cycle: The more pain we carry, the more effective we become at trading our pain and Christ's comfort for the healing of others. Then in turn, we receive an abundance of Christ's healing and joy. This is a sustainable healing model that provides life for both the survivor and the caregiver. We can most help sexually exploited youth as we embrace our own pain (whatever that might be), experience more of God's sufficiency, and thus know more intuitively how to embrace others in their pain and extend to them the healing power of Christ.

This process of healing cannot be rushed. As we demonstrate the necessary qualities of humility, warmth, welcome, authenticity, empathy, compassion, and gentle boldness, we will be the relational bridge to the healing love of Christ himself.

CHAPTER 1

∾

Princess Regina

Every little girl is a princess, and has something very special put inside of her that no one can take away. This is why each and every princess ever created must be protected and helped so that she can grow up and give the world all of the silvery sparkles that only she can give.

Princess Lost, *Introduction*

It is natural to feel overwhelmed when we think of the needs of exploited children and youth. They have experienced the most severe levels of trauma and life-threat, typically within the context of their most significant relationships. For most of these girls, their perpetrators have been the very people in their lives whom they most depended on for their basic needs: food, safety, shelter, and love. The breaking of these early relational bonds has shattered the foundation of trust for these girls. Tragically, their stories are layered narratives of deception and betrayal.

SYMPTOMS EXPERIENCED
BY ABUSE SURVIVORS

Because of the probability of deep levels of social betrayal (trusted authority figures that abuse) in early childhood, combined with numerous reoccurrences of life-threatening events, the sexually exploited girls that you serve will most likely experience the following symptoms.

Life-Threatening Events Most Often Produce:

1. **Anxiety/Fear.** Sexually exploited youth experience all kinds of life-threatening and dangerous events, including sexual and physical abuse, terror, captivity, profound neglect, and debilitating physical illness. A survivor's body and brain store these events, and remember them in complex, confusing, and intense ways. These body memories cause intensely high levels of anxiety and fear

that the survivor is not able to control. This is often her most pressing concern and issue.

2. **Depression.** Symptoms of depression in children and adolescents can include social withdrawal, intense anger or rage, disruptions in sleep and eating patterns, sadness, resignation, and despair.

3. **Anger.** This is a classic symptom of trauma and is actually a healthy reaction to abuse. Interpreting this anger as evidence that a survivor's soul is intact will be a helpful reframe for both of you in understanding this confusing emotion. Her anger demonstrates that she is still alive! In time, she will be able to control her outbursts as she is supported in addressing the underlying feelings, issues, and needs. Depending on the personality of the girl, her expressions of anger may serve as a guide in measuring her pain. Anger is typically triggered when she feels powerless, vulnerable, afraid, and/or trapped.

4. **Hyperarousal.** This is defined as "a condition in which the nervous system is perpetually aroused long after the traumatic event has ended. This results in chronic hypervigilance, anxiety, increased heart rate, sleeplessness, irritability, and even nausea."[20] What makes hyperarousal so confusing is that a seemingly endless number of events or experiences can unexpectedly (and often subconsciously) remind the brain of the trauma event and trigger a physiological response. The more these girls can be helped to understand this confusing bodily response, the less shame and more compassion they will feel toward

themselves. You may need to remind her of the complex effects of hyperarousal and encourage her with the truth that this is a *normal* response to the trauma she has experienced. She is not "crazy."

5. **Intrusive Memories.** Intrusion involves "the reliving of the trauma event through flashbacks when one is awake or through nightmares when one is asleep."[21] Intrusion can also create intense emotions, such as panic or rage. In practical terms, the trauma of the past keeps intruding into the present. As a result, the abuse victim has to keep reliving the event over and over again, often with the same vividness and emotional intensity of the original trauma.

Social Betrayal Most Often Produces:

1. **Dissociation.** The ability to "go away" within ourselves makes it possible to avoid painful events, recollections of those events, uncomfortable feelings, etc. Carol Gilligan describes it as the "ability to separate ourselves from parts of ourselves, to create a split within ourselves so that we can know and also not know what we know, feel and yet not feel our feelings."[22]

2. **Fragmentation.** Personality organization often becomes fragmented because of chronic childhood abuse. "Fragmentation in consciousness prevents the ordinary integration of knowledge, memory, emotional states, and bodily experience. Fragmentation in the inner representations of the self prevents the integrations of identity. Fragmentation in the inner representations of others prevents

the development of a reliable sense of independence within connection."[23] The effects of fragmentation largely explain why traumatized girls have difficulty trusting— themselves, you, or each other. It also explains why they fail to process information the same way that you might have done during your own healing. Normal adult communication requires both verbal abilities and abstract thinking skills; traumatized youth typically will not be able to process their trauma in a classic cognitive/behavioral manner. The brain will simply not allow it.

3. **Memory Impairment.** Abuse perpetrated by a trusted adult causes much higher levels of self-reported memory impairment than abuse perpetrated by a stranger. Typically, the memory of a child becomes disrupted at the time when the betrayal abuse begins. If there is not disclosure and loving intervention for this early abuse, then the child's ability to "take in" and learn becomes increasingly disrupted over time.

4. **Emotional Numbing.** This is the "shutting down of all feelings so that, instead of feeling pain, one simply feels nothing. Externally it has been described as a reduced responsiveness to the outside world."[24]

5. **Abusive or Controlling Relationships.** Because of significantly high levels of powerlessness, exploited and severely abused girls experience *trauma bonds* that harmfully connect them to the very ones who are abusing them. This is one of the most difficult effects of abuse/ trauma to understand and treat and is covered in detail in a later chapter.

Not only do these young survivors suffer from the complex and often debilitating symptoms of childhood abuse and trauma, they have also been impacted by the significant consequences of the sexualization of girls within our culture.

THE SEXUALIZATION OF OUR GIRLS

Not only do prostituted girls suffer the debilitating effects of abuse and betrayal trauma, they, like their non-trafficked peers, have been consistently sexualized in significant ways throughout most of their development. This sexualization is severely harmful to all girls. The American Psychological Association (APA) Task Force on the Sexualization of Girls was formed in response to expressions of public concern regarding the reality and impact of the increased sexualization of adolescent females. The following is drawn from the APA report.[25]

There are several components to sexualization that set it apart from healthy sexuality or development. Specifically, sexualization occurs when:

- A person's value comes only from his or her sexual appeal or behavior, to the exclusion of other characteristics.

- A person is held to a standard that equates physical attractiveness (narrowly defined) with being sexy.

- A person is sexually objectified—that is, made into a thing for others' sexual use, rather than seen as a person with the capacity for independent action and decision making.

• Sexuality is inappropriately imposed upon a person.

Only one of these conditions needs to be present as an indication of sexualization. However, the fourth condition (the inappropriate imposition of sexuality) is especially relevant to children. Anyone (girls, boys, men, women) can be sexualized. But when children are imbued with adult sexuality, it is imposed upon them rather than chosen by them. Self-motivated sexual exploration, on the other hand, is not sexualization by the APA's definition, nor is age-appropriate exposure to information about sexuality.

Nature of Sexualization

Virtually every media form studied provides ample evidence of the sexualization of young girls and women, including television, music videos, music lyrics, movies, magazines, sports media, video games, the Internet and advertising. The forms of media that are especially popular with children and adolescents, such as video games and teen-focused magazines, portray women (more often than men) dressed in revealing clothing, with bodily postures and facial gestures that imply sexual desire and readiness. These young girls are objectified and are often portrayed as decorative objects or as body parts rather than a whole person. Another disturbing aspect of this sexualization is the narrow and unrealistic standard of physical beauty that is emphasized and given to our girls for study and emulation. An example of this is the Bratz dolls that are dressed in sexualized clothing such as miniskirts, fishnet stockings, and feather boas. Thongs are now sized for seven- to ten-year-olds with various slogans such as "wink wink" and "spank me."

Societal messages that contribute to the sexualization of girls come not only from merchandise and the media but through their interpersonal relationships as well. Parents encourage sexualization by maintaining that physical beauty is the most important goal for girls. Some parents encourage plastic surgery, botox, and extreme diets to achieve these misguided goals.

Sadly, all girls in our culture are impacted by these messages but the sexually exploited girl is sexualized in more extreme ways. She has been repeatedly sexually assaulted (often by family members, coaches, or other trusted authority figures), dressed and taught to act in sexual ways, unprotected from pornography and other media images that depict women in sexually subservient roles to men, and often prostituted. *It doesn't take long for this sexualization to become her new identity and she in effect goes on to sexualize herself.* She is given much inspiration from the cultural landscape around her. As a part of her sexual victimization, she thinks of herself in objectified terms. Psychological researchers have identified *self-objectification as a key process whereby girls learn to think of and treat their own bodies as objects of others' desires.* In self-objectification, girls internalize an observer's perspective on their physical selves and learn to treat themselves as objects to be looked at and evaluated for their appearance. *This self-objectification exacerbates their vulnerabilities and increases their powerlessness as it makes them more dependent upon the men around them.*

Consequences of Sexualization

Sexualization has negative effects in a variety of domains, including cognitive functioning, physical and mental health, sexuality, attitudes, and beliefs.

- **Cognitive.** To the degree that young girls think about their bodies and compare themselves to cultural ideals they will likely develop cognitive distortions about their bodies, worth, interpersonal relationships, and sexuality.

- **Emotional.** Sexual objectification undermines confidence and diminishes emotional comfort with one's own body, leading to a host of negative emotional consequences, such as shame, anxiety, and self-disgust.

- **Mental and Physical Health.** *Research links sexualization with three of the most common mental health problems of girls and women—eating disorders, low self-esteem, and depression or depressed mood.*

- **Sexual.** Sexualization disrupts the healthy development of sexuality. Sexually exploited girls will have negative and/ or unrealistic expectations concerning sexuality. These negative effects most often lead to sexual dysfunction as adults. "More general societal effects may include an *increase in sexism,* … increased rates of sexual harassment and sexual violence, and an *increased demand for child pornography.*"

Implications for Mentors

- Provide media literacy training to educate survivors on the effects of their experiences both within the culture and as a result of forced prostitution. Teach critical skills in viewing and consuming media, focusing specifically on the sexualization of women and girls.

- Provide athletic opportunities and various extracurricular programs that offer alternative ways of identifying themselves as women.

- Provide comprehensive sexuality education. The girls must understand their bodies and the uniqueness of their design as women.

- Experience media with them in order to influence the way in which media messages are interpreted.

- Offer reparative education on God's view of them as women—their origins as unique image-bearers of him through their femininity. Emphasize individual differences in preferences, styles, and expressions as women. As they heal and address the lies they have been taught about their identity as women and the ways in which they are to be treated, they will uncover their own uniqueness and value. In time, their self-value and sense of personal worth will be transformed and restored.

- Give respect—expect respect—model respect.

Steps for Mentors

From the onset of the mentoring relationship focus primarily on *building trust* and *creating safety*. The following suggestions will get you started:

1. **Focus first on her basic personal and physical needs.** These would include medical needs, stable and safe living environment, treatment for addiction, and adequate food/clothing. To the degree that these are identified and met, she will experience increasing levels of stability and safety.

2. **Enter her world rather than requiring her to enter yours.** God modeled this most beautifully when he entered our world through Christ and was with us, experiencing our world with all its pain and suffering. He calls us to do the same.

3. **Demonstrate spiritual sensitivity.** Research tells us that she will probably have a history of religious abuse that will have shattered her basic trust in a "good God." It is critically important that you be sensitive to these issues without her having to initiate a conversation with you about it. This will go a long way in establishing an environment of safety (and eventually trust) between the two of you.

4. **Help her identify her most pressing emotional/psychological needs, including grief/loss, depression, fear/anxiety, anger, and shame.** You are not responsible to meet all these needs for her as that keeps her relationally

dependent and does not move her toward autonomy and self-empowerment. Instead, support her in identifying her most immediate needs, encourage her to ask for the specific support she desires, and then advocate for the additional help she is needing/requesting. For instance, if she confides in you that she is struggling significantly with anxiety and fear, you can connect her with resources for professional counseling if she so desires. Remember to *ask her* what she most needs instead of making these decisions for her. She will probably be either fiercely independent or overly dependent. In either case, she is most helped as you support her in developing her own autonomy and creating her own goals. This is best done through gentle coaching toward the balance of interdependence, which is a mutual dependence within a trusting relationship.

INTERACTIVE EXERCISE FOR THE GIRLS: OUTSIDE ME/INSIDE ME

Read chapter one of *Princess Lost* together, paying attention to the sections that evoke strong emotion. Have her note these in her journal so she can discuss later if she chooses. Affirm the importance of her thoughts and feelings and demonstrate a loving, nonjudgmental posture toward them. Her task is creating emotional connections; your role is to facilitate these connections, supporting her in appropriate emotional expression—both verbal and nonverbal. It might be helpful to discuss the following truths about feelings before you begin:

- Feelings are not right or wrong—they just are!

- Feelings are important to pay attention to, as they direct us to truth about our heart and/or our experiences.

- Feelings express our inner self; therefore, they are important.

- Feelings are numbed, blocked, and suppressed as an effect of trauma. It takes time and effort to begin to feel again.

- We must experience safety in order to feel.

- We cannot heal what we do not feel.

- We must feel in order to know what we need.

- Anger is a defensive emotion that sits on top of our deeper, more primary emotions: fear, hurt, or sorrow.

- It is normal to be afraid of feeling.

Encourage her to draw two pictures in her journal. The first picture is a self-portrait—the girl everyone sees on the outside. The second picture is the girl she can see on the inside— the girl nobody else can see. After completing these two pictures she can choose to share them or not, depending upon her readiness.

CHAPTER 2

∾

An Unexpected Scare

This was the first dark moment the princess had experienced,
and her tiny heart began to flutter.

Princess Lost, *Chapter 2*

One of the biggest challenges for those who have not experienced commercial sexual exploitation is trying to understand why girls choose to enter and remain in such a destructive lifestyle. Why would they choose to live with daily threats, beatings, and rapes? Pimps and johns are notoriously violent and misogynistic (female-hating). A significant percentage of pimps are diagnosable sociopaths. They are the most dangerous and twisted category of criminals, men whose consciences are so hardened that they have little or no ability to accept responsibility for their actions and who have lost all empathy for the pain of others. Biblical teaching on Satan gives great insights into these counterintuitive dynamics.

SATANIC STRATEGY: DECEPTION

Scripture tells us that a primary strategy Satan employs to destroy humans is deception. He is "a liar and the father of lies" (John 8:44). He deceives at both the micro and macro levels. He deceives nations and is the one "who leads the whole world astray" (Rev 12:9, 20:3). He also deceives individuals—believers and nonbelievers alike.[26] Some satanic lies connected with child sexual exploitation are obvious. For instance, sex traffickers often recruit poor, naive youth in majority-world countries through promises of jobs in another city or country. When the youth arrive at the destination, they are enslaved and forced into a life of prostitution. But much of the deception that empowers sexual exploitation is far more subtle and confusing, both for exploited youth and for their caregivers. As the "god of this world," Satan spreads many destructive lies about prostitution. These lies are influential in misleading youth into this destructive world. Such as: prostitution is a great way to make a lot of money; pimps are exciting people; only sexually repressed conservatives oppose prostitution, etc. In *Princess Lost*, Regina is intrigued with a goblin and says, "I think that beautiful creature likes me." She felt oddly drawn to him. Caregivers of sexually exploited youth often witness this dynamic at work. While it is disturbing that vulnerable girls are drawn to dangerous, evil men, it should not be surprising. The Apostle Paul said that Satan's workers operate through deception and often appear healthy and even godly, for "Satan himself masquerades as an angel of light" (2 Cor 11:14).

SATANIC STRATEGY: EXPLOITATION OF VULNERABILITIES

The Apostle Paul was not unaware of Satan's schemes (2 Cor 2:11), nor should we be ignorant of how Satan works to deceive and enslave exploited youth. Satan is crafty and nuances his deception based on our vulnerabilities. Exploited youth typically have numerous vulnerabilities that can be preyed upon: economic desperation due to chronic poverty and/or homelessness, naivety, emotional neediness due to a lack of parental love and affection, sexual susceptibility due to childhood abuse, etc. Proverbs 27:7 is very relevant here: "He who is full loathes honey, but to the hungry even what is bitter tastes sweet." This suggests that when girls' emotional and physical needs are met, they will not have insatiable craving. But if they are starved for male attention, a family, or basic sustenance, they may well find the most meager and putrid offers of relationship and care to "taste sweet."

Most pimps are experts at identifying and capitalizing on girls' vulnerabilities. For instance, detectives who specialize in commercial sexual exploitation speak of the "law of threes" pimps use, particularly in shopping malls, to recruit vulnerable youth into prostitution. When a pimp finds a group of three young girls, he will not target the most unattractive girl in the group, as she is less likely to believe his lines, nor will he target the most attractive girl for the same reason. But he will choose "girl number two," who is only moderately attractive, and tell her that she is beautiful, ask if she has ever considered modeling, and offer to help her get into modeling by taking some pictures in his photo studio. After some initial "normal" photos, he will tell her she could make a lot more money if she would do some more revealing photos. After that, he may blackmail her and threaten to post the revealing pictures online if she does not agree to have sex with some of his friends.

In the next section, we will discuss the effects of the trauma-bonding that occurs between youth and their abusers. However, it is worth noting here that young girls who have experienced abuse and neglect in childhood can be extremely vulnerable to charming and manipulative pimps who convince them that they love them. Even when the girl sees the "dark side" of the pimp, she is often unable or unwilling to acknowledge that he does not really love her—for this is all the "love" she has ever known. It is most painful for caregivers to watch helplessly as a survivor goes back again to a pimp who beats and abuses her, as soon as she gets out of jail or the hospital. Understanding that she has been deceived because of her deep, unmet needs and vulnerabilities helps us understand this dynamic. It also helps us begin to strategize how to support the survivor. Once her needs are met in healthy ways, she will be less vulnerable.[27]

IMPORTANCE OF LOVING, REPARATIVE RELATIONSHIPS

Secure attachments are vital for survival. The opposite is just as true. Broken or disturbed attachments in a child's early history are destructive, often to the point of death. Research tells us that sexually exploited children suffer from attachment disorders for multiple reasons. Most of them have experienced repeated traumatizing events (from multiple abusers) that prevent secure attachments from forming. They may have also endured addiction, abuse, and the loss of parent(s). They have likely lived in multiple homes and moved to and from multiple schools, all of which disrupts their stability and security. Young children do not have the frame of reference to identify trauma or abusive/abandoning experiences as unusual. They do not know that these early abuses or abandonments are *not the way relationships are supposed to be*. Thus, their brains internalize these disturbed bonds as normal.

The first natural bonding process between child and mother takes place in infancy, involving feeding and physical contact that form the basis of the infant's development of trust. The baby cries in distress, the mother comforts. Therefore, all "true bonding has elements of trauma, pain, difficulty, or uncertainty followed by gratification and/or relief. All true bonding involves an ordeal followed by success in the ... expressions of love or rescue by another."[28]

Bonding experiences take place in all kinds of situations, beginning with the mother-child bond. In these loving bonding routines, pain is followed by comfort and sustenance. In infant and childhood bonding, the child has physical and emotional needs that are met through milk, food, touch, movement, and eye contact, all of which the child learns to associate closely with love. In unhealthy bonding routines, pain is followed by negative outcomes.

Since the bonding cycle has been severely disrupted for these children, it must be repaired in corrective emotional interactions, experienced over and over again. These new comforting interactions occur within relationships known as *reparative relationships*—secure and stable nurturing relationships that are established and maintained within the healing community of the child. As you begin a caring relationship with a traumatized survivor, it will take her time to trust in the truth that, on any given day, you (or her abuser) will not come into her life (again) and hurt her. Most survivors stay on relational alert long after their abuse has stopped. The supportive relationship you initiate must be consistent and follow her development so that she can learn to trust again.

In summary, the corrective physical and emotional experiences (bonding routines) that your survivor most needs involve, in one way or another, an ordeal or challenge followed by feelings of relief, achievement, or gratification.[29]

Physical experiences

• Challenge/rope courses

• Wilderness experiences

• Team sports

Relational/emotional experiences

• Highly structured, highly loving foster and adoptive homes

• Loving and confrontative (truth) experiences within a relationship or group setting

• Solving challenges and problems together

THE DOUBLE BIND OF TRAUMATIZED GIRLS

Typically, traumatized children do not want to need or rely on others. However, they cannot meet their needs without doing so. Therefore, it is understandable why they might resent you. They need what you can do for them. In general, traumatized children (unlike healthy children) will avoid, fear, or push away the very people who really care about them. They will do this until they become convinced that you care about them and that you are in their lives to stay.

Conversely, these girls will most likely demonstrate a fierce loyalty to the very ones who have abused and exploited them:

> These children develop negative bonds that promote their survival, which are called loyalty bonds or trauma bonds. If someone holds your life in their hands, they are very relevant and powerful to you. Pleasing such a person, or at least not displeasing them, becomes critical. Such an experience can rapidly change an individual in lasting ways. The rape victim, the prisoner of war, the hostage, and the abused child all have similarities of experience.[30]

Therefore, these survivors will probably continue in the trauma bond long after the events are past. In a perverse way, the more severe and life-threatening the abuse, the stronger or more loyal the child will be to his or her abuser.

Research tells us that, as a result of failed early attachments, traumatized children typically demonstrate predictable symptoms. These could include:

- **Lack of basic trust**—the inability to show gratification, love, or affection.

- **Internalized rage and anger**—lack of self-respect and severe control problems.

- **Diminished conscience**—they have not internalized an "other." Thus, they have difficulty putting themselves in the shoes of another.

- **Development problems**—hoarding/gorging food, inability to demonstrate remorse, maladaptive emotional expression, etc.

- **Difficulty delaying gratification, impulsive, and reckless**— abused children learn that their world is unpredictable and thus they will probably not be helped or comforted. Contrast this to the belief system of children who have not experienced abuse or abandonment: "My world is predictable and loving; therefore I will be safe and cared for."

INTERACTIVE EXERCISE FOR THE GIRLS: FAMILY HISTORY/GENOGRAM

A genogram is a visual diagram or representation of a family. Although there is general agreement on the basic genogram structure and symbols, there are some variations from one author to another. Some authors reuse the same symbol for different situations, while others have ignored such special cases. GenoPro[31] has done meticulous research to determine what symbols and rules are best to create coherent genograms.

If you understand the following rules, you will be able to create complex genograms without much difficulty. The following are basic genogram symbols:

- The male is noted by a square and the female by a circle. A family is shown by a horizontal line connecting the two.

- The children are placed below the family line from oldest to youngest, left to right. Although this may sound obvious, it will be very important to remember these rules when the situation becomes a bit more complex.

- The male parent is placed to the left of the family and the female parent at the right.

- A spouse must be closer to his/her first partner, then the second partner (if any), third partner, and so on.

- The oldest child is at the left of the family, and the youngest child is at the right.

Sexually exploited children typically have complicated and chaotic family structures; therefore it is helpful and extremely validating for them to have a visual representation of this often painful and confusing family history. Your survivor may want to revisit this genogram and add to it as needed.

The following diagram is a fictional representation of one of these complex families. It will give you a visual example of how to create a genogram. This fictional female adolescent survivor, Hope, has an incarcerated biological father (who sexually abused her sister) and a mother who is currently divorcing Hope's stepfather. Hope has an older sister, younger sister, and two half siblings (a younger brother and sister). Her mother had three children by one man, and then divorced, marrying another man. Both sets of grandparents are still living. Hope has a living aunt and uncle on both sides of her family.

Hope used colored pencils in order to distinguish the "safe and caring" relatives from the others who have hurt her or hurt other members of her family. She selected a color for each of the following categories: drugs, promiscuous sex, prostitution, physical abuse, and sexual abuse, and then made a color graph on the bottom of the page. She chose a purple arrow to depict the perpetration of abuse by one member of her family upon another member.

This family exercise is important for a survivor because it helps her have a visual representation of the inter-generational patterns of abuse victimization, incarceration, prostitution, and perpetration of abuse. After completing this exercise (it took several weeks to finish), Hope was better able to identify the "safe" and "not safe" members of her family. This exercise was clarifying and validating in other ways also, as it helped her not only to understand the inter-generational patterns of abuse in her family of origin, but also to recognize the positive influences of loving and nurturing members of her immediate and extended family. After completing this exercise, she felt clearer and more empowered to set some boundaries for herself with various family members.

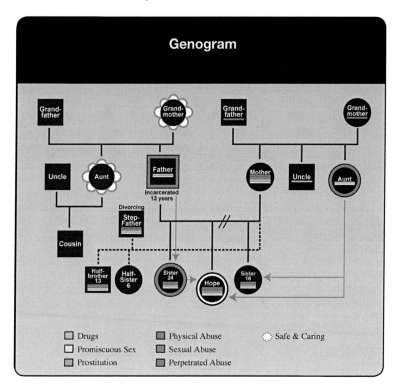

Practice creating genograms until you are comfortable with the rules and the use of this tool. You can practice with your own family if you would like. There is a blank, bordered page titled "My Family" in the *Princess Lost Journal*, where a survivor can create her own family history. Because this is a complex and involved exercise, allow several weeks or sessions for this exercise to be completed.

It is important not to rush this process. Most often a survivor will want to discuss the various relationships she is visually representing in this exercise. Listen and ask good questions as she draws; offer her quality, focused attention. I have found that girls do not want to be alone when they are completing this exercise and thus, will most enjoy this time if they can do it with you or in a small group.

Follow her promptings and ask clarifying questions. As you listen, reflect back to her the things you are hearing. For example, "I want to make sure I am understanding you well. It sounds like you are saying that you hate it when your mother lies to you about her history of prostitution and that is why you like talking honestly to me about the things you have done and experienced even though it is difficult. Is that correct?"

Following are some suggestions for good reflective questions:

- Would you like to talk about your father (mother, brother, sister, etc.)?

- What would you like me to know about him/about your relationship with him?

- What do you think is important to remember about him? How shall we represent that on your genogram?

- Who felt safest to you? What made them feel safe? How would you like to draw that on your genogram?

- Tell me about your mother. Who was she closest to?

- Who felt most like a mother to you growing up? Tell me about her.

- What did your mother teach you about men? About love? About yourself?

- If you could change one thing about your family, what would it be?

- If you had a magic wand and could make three wishes, what would you wish for?

After completing the genogram, use colored pencils and suggest the following activities:

1. Pick a color that reminds you of safety and love. Color the shape of the person who was the safest and most nurturing in your family. "How does thinking about this person make you feel?"

2. Pick another color that reminds you of fear and pain. Color the shape of the person(s) who has hurt you the most in your family. "How does thinking about this person make you feel?"

3. Pick a color for physical abuse, sexual abuse, prostitution, drugs/alcohol, promiscuous sex. Draw a line under the shape of the person(s) who has experienced these things.

CHAPTER 3

∾

Encountering Whistler

He was the Whistler they had heard so much about in the village.
His were the tunes that the villagers lived by,
tunes that seemed to possess a power that defied all rational explanation.
His songs quietly guided and comforted,
and because of this, the boy was loved by all.

Princess Lost, *Chapter 3*

> The Holy Scriptures are our [love] letters
> from home. I have read in Plato and Cicero
> sayings that are wise and very beautiful; but I
> have never read in either of them: Come unto
> me all ye that labor and are heavy laden.
> —ST. AUGUSTINE

Augustine was an extremely influential, godly African church leader in the late fourth and early fifth century. Throughout his life he faced much human and demonic challenge and opposition. As he lay dying in the city of Hippo (in present-day Algeria), the Vandals, a Barbarian eastern Germanic tribe, had laid siege to the city and would soon sack it. Augustine asked to have several of the Psalms of David put on the wall next to his bed. He spent his final days on Earth the way he had spent most of his Christian life—praying and meditating on Scripture.

SCRIPTURE AND SPIRITUAL WARFARE

Chapter three of *Princess Lost* introduces Whistler, a metaphor for the Holy Spirit, who sings two songs that frighten away the goblins. These songs are based on two Scripture passages.
    Whistler's first song is below:

> *Go and tell! Go and tell!*
> *The goblins will be stomped,*
> *The wicked will be stopped.*
> *The curse will lift,*
> *The lame will skip,*
> *The blind will see,*
> *The poor will eat,*

The deaf will hear,
The goons will fear.
Go and tell! Go and tell!
The sick are healed,
The dead are raised.
Go and tell!

This first song is based on Matthew 11:2–5, below:

When John heard in prison what Christ was
doing, he sent his disciples to ask him, "Are you
the one who was to come, or should we expect
someone else?" Jesus replied, "Go back and report
to John what you hear and see: The blind receive
sight, the lame walk, those who have leprosy are
cured, the deaf hear, the dead are raised, and the
good news is preached to the poor.
MATTHEW 11:2–5

Whistler's second song is as follows:

There you go in a fury
Never more in a hurry,
Worthless and wicked,
Devious and shrewd,
You will be devoured!
And you don't know the hour,
Off you go in a fury!

This second song is based on Psalms 18:25–27, below:

To the faithful you show yourself faithful,
to the blameless you show yourself blameless,
to the pure you show yourself pure,
but to the crooked you show yourself shrewd.
You save the humble but bring low those whose
eyes are haughty.

Scripture is essential in our battle against satanic forces. In Paul's great treatise on spiritual warfare, he reminds us that "our struggle is not against flesh and blood, but against the rulers, against the authorities, against the powers of this dark world and against the spiritual forces of evil in the heavenly realms" (Eph 6:12). Though our enemy has great power, we are not dependent on our own strength to defeat him. In fact, Paul begins this passage on an extremely encouraging note: "Finally, be strong in the Lord and in his mighty power" (Eph 6:10).

Pippety was rightfully afraid of the goblins, but she sadly failed to understand the powerful weapons right in front of her. When Paul lists our resources for spiritual battle, the only offensive weapon he identifies is "the sword of the Spirit, which is the word of God" (Eph 6:1). Our Lord himself modeled this when he was personally, directly tempted by Satan in the wilderness. Three times in a row Jesus cited Scripture to refute Satan's deceitful attacks (Matt 4:1–11).

Using Scripture in our battle against Satan is more than simply quoting Bible verses out loud. Satan himself misquoted Scripture when tempting Jesus. Rather, using "the sword of the Spirit" means that we faithfully, reflectively meditate on Scripture so that we know it well and build our lives on its truths. Then, when we face attacks from Satan, we use specific, appropriate Scripture to counter Satan's attack. Using "specific, appropriate Scripture" is based on the Greek word Paul uses when he describes Scripture as the *sword* of the Spirit. There are two Greek words for sword in the New Testament. One was the *rhomphaia*, the large, heavy sword soldiers would bring down on their opponents with great force—just as some Christians seem to think that overwhelming people (or Satan) with a dump-truck load of Scripture passages will give victory.

However, Paul does not describe the sword of the Spirit as the large, heavy *rhomphaia*. Rather, he uses a different Greek word for sword, the *makaira*, which refers to a short dagger. A Roman soldier would use his heavy, broad-blade sword to pound the opponent, but, once he got in close, he would look for the specific opening in the enemy's armor and pierce him in that precise spot with his dagger. Thus, Paul is saying that we are to use God's Word in specific, targeted ways to counter Satan's lies.

As mentors, one of the best ways to do this is to make extensive use of Scripture in your own life. You will grow increasingly proficient at exercising the sword of the Spirit to counter Satan's lies. As you do, you can then humbly and gently assist your survivor, showing her what it looks like to apply God's Word in precise ways and in specific times of need. This requires knowing Scripture well *and* knowing well the person you are serving.

THE HOLY SPIRIT AND SPIRITUAL WARFARE

In *Princess Lost*, Whistler represents the Holy Spirit. His songs represent the Word of God. When we came to Christ,

God the Father "delivered us from the dominion of darkness and transferred us to the kingdom of his beloved Son" (Col 1:13 RSV). Thus, the believer belongs to Christ, not to Satan, and has a new power to be victorious over demonic forces. This power comes from God, who at the point of our conversion gives us the Spirit to permanently indwell us (Eph 1:13–14). The Spirit is the author of Scripture. He is the one who guided the human authors to write the very words of God (1 Pet 1:20–21). And he is the one who illuminates the Scriptures by working in the hearts of believers. He helps us understand and apply God's truth (John 14:16–17, 1 Cor 2:12–14). Furthermore, the Holy Spirit aids us in our battle against Satan by:

- Guiding us in ministry (Rom 8:14)

- Giving help in time of need, for he is the "comforter" sent by Christ to help us (John 14:16)

- Empowering us in fruitful ministry, allowing us to have an effective witness to unbelievers (Acts 1:8, 4:8)

- Empowering us to have victory over sin (Rom 8:13–14, Gal 5:16)

- Living "by the Spirit" (Gal 5:16, 25). That is, we must live by *his* strength, being responsive and obedient to his leading

SPIRITUAL CARE OF SEXUALLY EXPLOITED GIRLS

All people are spiritual beings. As a part of a holistic approach to healing, we must include the emotional and spiritual needs of the women and children rescued. In faith-based aftercare programs, spiritual care is a top priority, because it is the healing power of Christ that transforms and redeems the broken. We cannot fully emancipate these young survivors until they have emotionally healed and been spiritually restored. The only true redemption for their hearts and souls is experiential knowledge of a God who loves them individually, forgives them, and has a plan for their healing, restoration, and redemption. God's love is the only tonic for toxic shame. He is the only one who can give every survivor a new identity and life purpose. The survivor will come to experience God as a "good" God as she experiences good and sacrificially loving relationships.

Sexual exploitation not only distorts a survivor's perception of herself and others, but also her concept of God. Most likely, her perception of God is filtered through her experiences with previous male authority figures and her relationships with them. Many of these exploited girls will not have even one safe, nurturing male relationship in their attachment histories. Therefore, the most effective, transformational spiritual care will be the consistent, loving interactions the girls have with you and other caregivers.

The following diagram addresses the common distortions that sexual abuse survivors have of God, self, and others:

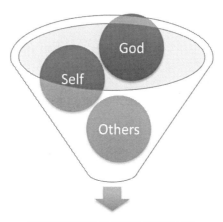

HEALTHY RELATIONAL INTIMACY

A Distorted View of God

• God is uncaring

• God is manipulative and exploitive

• God is narcissistic

• God is untrustworthy

• God is distant and uncaring

A Distorted View of Self

- Undeveloped sense of personal identity

- Inferior and inadequate

- Hard and tough on the outside

- Powerless and defenseless

- Feel dirty and full of shame

- Objectified with no sense of value or personal dignity

- Self hate: don't know how to love or care for myself: Hate self

- Guilty: I did something wrong

- Unworthy of a better lifestyle

- Self punishing: believe that I deserve to be treated abusively: It is my punishment

A Distorted View of Others

- Inability to trust: trust has been violated by everyone who has promised to take care me: family/friends/pimps/buyers

- Suspicious, cautious

- Walls built around me to keep others from really knowing me

- Assume others are against me

- Manipulative, deceptive patterns of relating that are/ were necessary for survival

- Emotionally precocious: survival depended upon my ability to scan an environment and to deliver what was expected of me

- Sexualized: associate closeness and love with sex

In a very real sense, you are the most important spiritual care resource for your survivor. She must see and experience the reality and power of God in your life. This kind of incarnational witness, based on the life of Christ (John 1:14), is much more demanding, yet infinitely more powerful, than mere spiritual activities in a weekly program. Hence, it is imperative that staff and mentors are godly, personally healthy, and well trained to minister to survivors.[32]

Research tells us that the vast majority of abuse survivors, prostituted minors, and homeless youth value spirituality and are open to—and even desire—faith-based resources for their recovery. However, *it is imperative to be sensitive, gentle, and cautious in providing spiritual care to this population of adolescents.* They have been systematically exploited by those who said they wanted to help them. Many have been sexually abused by parents and johns who were professing Christians. Some have been spiritually abused by pimps and other authority figures. Many prostituted girls have had buyers they knew who were pastors or lay church leaders—men who paid to degradingly abuse their bodies on Friday night and then stepped to the pulpit on Sunday morning to proclaim "the truth of Scripture." Those of us who have not had this experience cannot understand the spiritual damage and confusion created when a girl's father beats her mother (or her), stating that he did it because she "wasn't submissive as God says women must be," or when a pimp who viciously beats and gang-rapes the girls in his "stable" talks about God, goes to church, or even quotes Scripture. These are unfortunately common experiences for some prostituted girls.

The survivor typically will feel ready for spiritual help when she has experienced the steadfast genuineness, integrity, and unconditional love of staff and mentors who love Jesus. Once she is ready for spiritual help, the following spiritual topics need to be covered, patiently and with sensitivity:

- Perceiving God as a loving Father: Undoing the distortions created by abusive father figures who have exploited her; for example, pimps who refer to themselves as "daddy" or "husband," etc.

- Biblical (healthy) sexuality versus cultural/pornographic sexuality[34]

- Role of the Holy Spirit versus demonic activity

- Soul care, prayer, and healing meditation

- Dangerous relationships versus loving, safe relationships

- Connecting again—with self, God, and others

- Committed friendships—safe people versus dangerous people

- Healthy emotional expression versus unmitigated anger

- Forgiveness—the final stage of healing

- Specific soul care tools/skills

- Scripture as source of truth, guidance, and comfort

- Armor of God and victory over Satan

IMPLICATIONS FOR MENTORS

In summary, the spiritual needs of abuse survivors are manifold and complex. Children rescued from sexual exploitation and prostitution have even greater spiritual needs due to the spiritually distorted environments they have experienced. Their view of God has been misshaped in critical developmental stages through the abusive, traumatic, and exploitive interactions they have endured with men who have authority over them. It is critical that mentors remember:

1. Your divine mandate is to love in Jesus's name, not to convert.

2. It is the Spirit of God who convicts, draws people's hearts, and gives spiritual life (John 3:5, 16:8–11).

3. The love and care offered the survivor in Jesus's name will point the way to Christ.

4. God's constant faithfulness and sweet presence, through the Spirit, will strengthen a survivor to have faith in Christ.

5. Many seeds will be planted in her heart along the way.

Gently address the topic of spirituality that is introduced in chapter three of *Princess Lost*. Allow the survivor to share with you the comfort level she has pertaining to her spirituality. Tell her that your priority is to create a safe place for her, emotionally and spiritually. Together, develop a specific list of guidelines based on her vulnerabilities and spiritual needs.

To illustrate, I want to share a story about a young survivor whom I'll call Hope.[35] She was healing from early childhood abuse, homelessness, and subsequent sexual exploitation. Religion felt very unsafe to her.

Early in our therapeutic relationship, we discussed her spiritual needs. When I asked what she needed to feel emotionally and spiritually safe, Hope immediately requested two things: no direct or indirect discussions about God, and definitely no prayer. She went on to describe how girls "like her" were really good at giving others what they expected and wanted, that she desperately needed a relationship with me where she could be bluntly honest about what she felt and thought spiritually. I assured her that I had full confidence in her healing journey and that I trusted her with the truth about what she was ready for in our relationship. Six months after this conversation, I received the following text from Hope, a poignant example of the Spirit's power to make himself known to survivors—no matter how resistant they might seem to the Gospel:

> I have been doing some meditating today and
> have decided that you are my great guide …
> Thank you for bringing me home.

INTERACTIVE EXERCISE FOR THE GIRLS: IMAGING GOD

Read aloud chapter three in *Princess Lost.* Encourage your survivor to pay attention to the sections that evoke strong emotion. Have her note these in her journal so she can talk about them if she chooses. Affirm the importance of her thoughts and feelings and of your nonjudgmental posture toward them. Her task is creating emotional connections; your role is to facilitate these connections by coaching her in appropriate emotional expressions—verbal and nonverbal. It might be helpful to communicate the following:

- She is created as a spiritual being.

- You desire for her to feel safe spiritually so that she can fully heal.

- You need to know what does and does not feel spiritually safe to her so that you can attune your responses to her in such a way that they will not be triggering.

Invite her to share with you her spiritual history. How has faith been taught and/or modeled to her? How has she been helped spiritually? How has she been hurt spiritually? Is she aware of any current spiritual needs? Does she want to make any specific requests?

Encourage the use of her journal for this exercise because there are probably memories and feelings that she is not ready to share. If she writes them down now, she can come back to them and share them when she feels ready.

Encourage her to draw a picture of God in her journal and share it if she would like to. Ask her to tell you about her drawing and then ask specific questions based on your observations of her picture. Depending upon her readiness and felt spiritual needs, share with her some of the truths from this chapter on the spiritual world and the role of the Holy Spirit. Remember to be extremely sensitive to the oppression she has experienced and her history of spiritual abuse. As she feels increasingly loved and safe, she will ask for more spiritual guidance from you. Wait for her promptings and continue to courageously listen to her, attuning your responses to what you are hearing. The Spirit of God is the one who is powerfully working within her, drawing her heart toward the love of Christ.

CHAPTER 4

〜

The Princess and Her Papa King

Regina was sad that her Papa King had to leave.
She didn't quite understand where he had to go or what he had to do,
but she trusted him to always come back to her.
One thing she knew for certain was that he loved her with an unfailing love.
She was precious to him, and she knew it.

Princess Lost, *Chapter 4*

For many girls, this chapter will trigger grief as they read about the princess and her intimate relationship with her Papa. It also might prompt memories of an early childhood before abuse and subsequent life on the streets. Because of her history of early abuse and exploitation, your survivor will be reminded of the many things and relationships that she has lost. Grief is a natural and important part of her healing and will begin to manifest as she feels safe and begins to stabilize physically and psychologically.

GRIEF: AN ACT OF GREAT COURAGE

Grief is not a one-time event, but a process of remembering, feeling, and expressing. Young survivors have experienced years of loss and, therefore, grieving will unfold over time, although the amount of time will differ from girl to girl. The grief process may take two to three years for adults and sometimes even longer for children. It is helpful to understand the basic tasks of grief as you offer care. She must be able to:

1. Understand the loss(es)

2. Itemize the loss(es)

3. Feel the loss(es)

4. Express the feelings of loss

5. Commemorate the loss(es)

6. Find meaning in the loss(es)

Before addressing the grief process with a survivor, invest some time in empathically understanding and feeling the deep, numerous losses she has endured. This will prepare you to sensitively listen and validate her as she shares these losses with you. When she does share, listen and feel with her. These repeated interactions will create emotional and psychological connections for her. As she builds relational trust, she will share and feel more with you, each time feeling less isolated and less alone. This is, in essence, the healing process. It is not a one-time event, but a process of grieving (feeling pain connected to painful events, expressing the feelings experienced, and receiving comfort) that will continue for years. The best mentors are caregivers built into the real-life community of the survivor.

UNDERSTANDING AND RESPONDING TO ANGER AS GRIEF

As a survivor experiences physical and psychological safety, she will begin to thaw emotionally and express her feelings more freely. It is not uncommon for adolescents initially to express their grief through anger and rage. This can be overwhelming and disconcerting for mentors to hear. You might be tempted to shut down this expression of anger or repress it in some way. Instead, allow it and validate the anger as a measurement of her pain: deep, visceral, and real. Don't judge her, but allow the anger to be felt and expressed. She needs to hear that you also feel angry about the pain she has and continues to experience.

The survivor will need encouragement and support in expanding her expressive skills in the grief process. For instance, she might be stuck in anger and will have a very limited emotional vocabulary. She may lack the verbal tools to talk specifically about the things that have happened to her or to express how she feels about them. Encourage and support the artistic, emotional expressions of drawing, painting, dance, and clay. These activities can be done together or separately, depending upon the personality and desires of the girl. Encourage the girl to talk about her art, poetry, or dance and ask questions that encourage further processing, such as:

- What were you feeling when you were painting this picture?

- What do you want to tell me about your picture?

- When you look at your picture, what do you see?

- Does this picture surprise you in any way?

- What are you feeling now?

- May I tell you what I see and feel when I look at your picture?

- How do you feel now after drawing and talking about your picture?

- Thank you for sharing your picture with me.

These questions will move your survivor through the grief process as she is supported in feeling and, thus, rescheduling her losses. When a survivor draws and/or paints, she creates a level of mastery over the overwhelming emotion she feels. This process gives her some relief through emotional release. In time, these repeated expressions of grief, followed by comfort within a safe relationship, will result in healing. This is a natural process—one that the Spirit of God will mediate and guide.

Appendix D contains two feeling charts: one with words and one with feeling faces. Encourage the use of these tools to expand her emotional vocabulary.

A THEOLOGY OF REMEMBRANCE AND MOURNING

American Christians are generally unaccustomed to remembering and mourning losses as a positive exercise, let alone as an act of worship. However, it is actually unhealthy and ungodly to gloss over, deny, or repress major losses and the painful feelings that accompany them. For maximum healing and growth, we need a process by which we systematically articulate our painful losses and grieve them. This keeps us from distorting reality and shutting down emotionally. It can also drive us to God in the midst of our pain and confusion. Note, for instance, how the following godly individuals in Scripture responded to catastrophic losses:

The Jewish exiles had been deported to Babylon and, remembering the destruction of their homeland, they wept. They cried out in an oath saying, "Let my tongue cleave to the roof of my mouth, if I do not remember you, if I do not set Jerusalem above my highest joy!" (Ps 137:6 RSV).

After Job lost his children and possessions, he tore his clothes and shaved his head as a sign of mourning. He also articulated his losses to God: "The Lord gave and the Lord has taken away" (Job 1:21).

Jesus wept over the inhabitants of Jerusalem and over their impending loss of life and destruction. He is painfully and graphically specific in articulating these losses, including the slaughter of children by being dashed to the ground (Luke 19:41–44).

The prophet Jeremiah repeatedly remembered and grieved over the multitude of physical and spiritual losses, present and future, that resulted from Israel's rebellion and failure to turn back to God. "Oh, that my head were a spring of water and my eyes a fountain of tears! I would weep day and night for the slain of my people" (Jer 9:1).

Remembering and grieving losses is such an important process that an entire book of the Bible—Lamentations— is dedicated to this. Jeremiah probably wrote this short Old Testament book after the violent destruction of Jerusalem by the Babylonians. Lamentations records numerous specific losses in detail and does not shrink back from recounting ugly, graphic events such as the rape of women and torture of town leaders (Lam 5:11–12), the starvation of children and their cannibalism by their own parents (2:11–12, 4:10), and the slaughter of men, women, and children. Lamentations specifically recounts and mourns the loss of ability to worship, the loss of dignity before enemies, children's loss of parents, the loss of city and homeland. Their further losses included:

- Loss of freedom

- Loss of virginity

- Loss of joy

- Loss of peace and happiness

- Loss of health

- Loss of life[36]

To this day, faithful Jews read the book of Lamentations on Tisha b'Av, the annual day of fasting, to remember the destruction of Jerusalem in 586 BC.

The Complex Grief of Exploited Girls

The following list shows some of the numerous and complex losses experienced by a sexually exploited child:[37]

- The loss of her life before she was abused/exploited

- The loss of the way that things "should have been"

- The loss of relationships before abuse/exploitation

- The loss of relationships she came to know and care for during captivity

- Inability to return home because it is not safe or for cultural reasons

- The loss of virginity, childhood innocence, and "timelessness"

- The loss of belief in a safe world (being beaten or watching others she loved be beaten or murdered)

- Submitting to shameful and humiliating behaviors to avoid being beaten or killed

- Death of people she knew and loved

- The loss of childhood—the developmentally normal experiences of graduating from high school, playing sports, joining clubs, celebrating birthdays, and play

- The loss of nurture and comfort

- The loss of healthy dating and courting experiences, falling in love, and marriage to a man who is safe and loving

- The loss of her faith in a "good" God and "good" people

- The loss of the development of skills and talents

These young survivors have experienced incalculable losses. There is *so very much for these girls to mourn.* Therefore, we must be patient, understanding, and thoughtful as she begins to awaken her heart to these losses. We must also be careful and cautious, not using glib expressions of reassurance that might feel invalidating and insensitive in lieu of all she has suffered and experienced. Do not say, for instance, "It will be okay," "I know what you are feeling," or "You'll get over it." We *do not* know precisely what she is feeling, or has experienced, and, in a very real way, she will never completely get over it this side of heaven. Chances are that there are losses she will never tell anybody in a lifetime. We are there to help her move through the grief, to offer comfort and presence. This is a sacred process. Our best responses are to listen, to ask questions that draw out her heart, to feel with her, and to validate her experiences as tragic, awful, and real.

As she remembers, the need to preserve safety must constantly be balanced against the need to face the past. Her intrusive symptoms[38] should be monitored carefully so that she is able to maintain a sense of safety, feeling grounded to the present while gradually facing the horrific reality of the past.

During this time, it is normal for her to be unable to function at the highest level of her ability. Reassure her that, once this work of remembering and mourning is behind her, she will feel a sense of restored stamina, energy, and focus. Your survivor will not be able to do this uncovering work while she is dealing with immediate life crises or distracted by other important life goals.

Talk with her about her pressing needs and discuss together the best time for her to enter into this part of her healing. Tell her that she will not have to do this work alone; have her write down the names of safe people in her life who can feel and grieve with her. Be clear about the time and energy that you can offer her. Because it is difficult for her to trust, schedule time (two to three hours per visit is best) that will work for both of you and be consistent with follow-through. She will eventually learn to trust you as she experiences you as trustworthy.

ANCHOR OBJECTS: SOOTHING IMAGERY

Safe anchors are soothing images or objects that evoke feelings of comfort and love. These are objects or pictures that a survivor can keep with her to anchor her to feelings of security and safety when she is feeling overwhelmed with intrusive traumatic imagery. If possible, help the survivor find an image(s) of safe relationships that have been preserved from her past. Even one or two memories of a caring person from childhood will give her hope and courage to push on through her grief. Healing art or framed images from *Princess Lost* can also serve as anchors that remind her of her worthiness, value, and capacity to love and be loved.[39] A secure sense of connection with caring people will, in time, provide the eventual, powerful foundation for her recovered sense of personality. Following are some questions/suggestions that come out of attachment theory and will further a secure connection between you and the survivor you are mentoring:

- Ask yourself, "How can I best use myself as a healing instrument that maximizes the adolescent's ability to develop a good attachment relationship, not only with me, but also with his or her current parents and caregivers?"[40]

- Remind her that she is not alone—that you are committed to her and her healing.

- Encourage her to write down the names and phone numbers of two people she can call if she is alone and suddenly needs comfort and support.

- Offer high levels of verbal and written affirmation and reassurances.

- Consistently "check in" regarding her safety needs.

- When you observe glimpses of her originally designed self, reflect this back to her so she can begin to see herself in this new light.

The survivor's attachment history will direct her interactions with you. For example, boundary-less girls (those with disorganized attachments) will need you to relate out of your own clear boundaries so that you can provide the appropriate, predictable, and loving environment needed by the girl for her to experience a relationally secure base.

If a survivor is aggressive, she might be trying to provoke anger in you. It is important that you consistently relate to her in a directly honest, kind, calm, and loving manner, which will create a new, healthier script for her. She is expecting your anger and rejection. That is why she works so hard to create this abandoning response in you. Your consistent emotional availability will, in time, form a secure, loving foundation for her to connect to. It will be life-changing for her to experience both your love and your honesty/firmness at the same time.

An example of these principles is illustrated in Celestia's experience with a young girl named Vanessa:

Months after I had initiated a mentoring relationship with a young exploited girl in one of our local juvenile detention facilities, she was released to the streets the day she turned 18. Weeks later, Vanessa called me, clearly agitated and triggered. Her voice was twitchy and sharp as she responded to my eager initiation of support and questions about how I could help her.

"F*** you, Celestia! F*** you! Why do you love me so much?" Vanessa's voice bit like a knife.

I was stunned and taken aback by this explosion. I had never been asked this question before in this manner! I was quiet until I could think of a good reply, "I just do … I can't help myself. I guess I never lose track of who you were created to be."

"F*** you!" Clearly this conversation wasn't going well. I stumbled over my words, not sure of the best response. Vanessa was too triggered to talk.

I concluded our conversation by saying, "I love you, Vanessa. There is nothing you can do to push me away. I am here for you when you need me. I love you."

I hung up stunned. This had never happened to me before in my comfortable and predictable private practice. I had no script! Something deep within told me that Vanessa was afraid. She was afraid that I might leave her like the rest of her family had. She was afraid that she might just trust me and then I would fail her too, rejecting her or abandoning her like everybody else in her life had done. The one thing I knew was that I must not let her strategy of behaving "awful" work; I must not allow her to push me away. I texted her, "Vanessa, I love you and am here when you feel ready to talk."

Days later my phone rang again. It was Vanessa. Again, minutes into our conversation she'd triggered, erupting into violent rage. I had never heard such a barrage of cursing from such a tiny girl. I stayed on the phone with her, trying to calm her down. I was mildly successful. Clearly, this was becoming our new pattern of dialogue. The next time she called I cautiously initiated another strategy.

"Hey, Vanessa."

"Yes?"

"You know how I'm always honest with you, right?"

"Yea, I guess."

"Well, there's something I want to tell you that might be hard for you to hear, but I want you to try to understand. I'm sorry that you've been hurt so much in the past. I'm sorry that you've been cussed at and verbally humiliated by so many people. That's actually called abuse—it's verbal abuse and it hurts. It hurts to be treated that way. I know it hurts you and it hurts me. I won't ever treat you that way because I don't want you to hurt either. I know you don't want to hurt me but I think you might be scared, and that's why you're pushing me away with your words. So, let's practice something, okay?"

"Okay, what?" She's stunned by my "bold words," as she calls them.

"When you call and I answer the phone, I will say, 'Well, hello, Vanessa. How can I help you today?' " I exaggerated my voice, as I role-played another kind of dialogue. She giggled and I heard the first hint of that little girl locked carefully away.

"Then what do I do?" she asked, getting into our new game. It's clearly a relief to have me address the cussing-rut we've been in.

"Then you practice making a request or telling me something I might not know about you for that day and how you're feeling. Okay, let's practice. Ring. Ring. 'Hello? Is this Vanessa?'"

She giggled, and we had our first good conversation since she was released from jail.

Today, as I edit this manuscript it's ten months later. Following this loving, respectful, but honest interaction Vanessa never spoke disrespectfully to me again. After four failed intakes in local shelters she has been successfully placed and is working in a residential program. She continues to stay in touch, often daily with several of our MTS mentors. This "confrontation" was foundational to building a bridge of trust within our community.

During one of my recent visits, I had another breakthrough conversation with Vanessa as we sat on her bed. She started talking about her remorse in hurting the ones whom she knows have loved her most in her life

(MTS mentors). This opened up an amazing opportunity for her to identify and pay attention to the emotions she was experiencing—as I described the various possible feelings, she knew immediately it was guilt. For the first time in nine months she allowed me to show her in the Scriptures where God talks about guilt—why we have it, and what we are to do with it. We also talked about love—true love—the kind that we experience when others sacrifice for us. She asked about God's love and we talked about his sacrifice for her, all for love. She was quiet and asked me to pray for her. Then she asked me to bring her another Bible (her "boyfriend" threw out her previous ones). This story is an example of the natural opportunities we'll have, as we love the girls God has given to us—both in truth and in grace.

A final principle in becoming a healing instrument to sexually exploited girls is to develop a sense of "we-ness" with the survivor. Small gifts, a picture of the two of you together (which provides a visible symbol of connection), and occasional phone calls will more quickly facilitate a connection. These anchors are important, as she has not yet internalized a belief that she is loved.

PAPA KING: THE CHARACTER OF GOD

One of the most difficult losses experienced by survivors of abuse and exploitation is the loss of confidence in God as a loving heavenly Father who can be trusted. When fellow humans abuse their power against us, it is frightening to think of relating to God, the ultimate authority; it's anything but soothing. This difficulty is sharply compounded for young girls who have been abused or exploited by their father or a father figure, since Scripture speaks of God as our heavenly Father.[41] Some theological liberals have responded to this challenge by essentially dismissing the concept of God as a heavenly Father. John Cooper's comments are very helpful here:

> It is also true that many people in our culture (and others) have difficulty relating to a Father God if they lack experience of a good father. ... But for most people, the need, desire, and ability to relate to a father figure is still strongly present. Many people who lack good human fathers gladly and readily receive God the Father as their ultimate security and source of healing. Eliminating the Heavenly Father is neither necessary nor helpful for dealing with the sins of their earthly fathers.[42]

We strongly agree with Cooper that people have an innate longing for a healthy father figure. God has built this into the human heart. Every young woman deserves to have an experience of an earthly father and a heavenly Father such as that described in chapter four of *Princess Lost*. Satan, the deceiver and destroyer, loves to pervert our understanding of God's attributes. Therefore, caregivers must be very sensitive to exploited girls' perceptions of God, particularly as a heavenly Father, and gently assist them in reimaging God. Caregivers must gently correct distortions about the fatherhood of God. Healthy conceptions and images of God, based on biblical truth, are most important for healing and spiritual health.

When it's appropriate, review some of the beautiful biblical pictures and descriptions of our heavenly Father. This is one of the most powerful methods for correcting a distorted image of God. When you do review these biblical "father" passages, highlight the tender, loving, and unconditional qualities that exploited girls have not experienced from earthly father figures. For instance:

- He feeds and cares for the birds of the sky, and has infinitely more loving concern for the sexually exploited girl than for the birds (Matt 6:26).

- He delights in giving good gifts to us, regardless of our performance. Further, he delights in this even more than the best of human fathers (Matt 7:11).

- He knows and notices when a tiny sparrow falls from the sky. He knows and cares when we suffer (Matt 10:29).

- He so actively and passionately cares for us that no detail of our lives is overlooked or ignored by him. He even keeps track of the very number of hairs on our heads (Matt 10:29–31).

- He tenderly loves the powerless and the vulnerable. He delights in hiding truth from arrogant powerful authorities and graciously revealing it to those who resemble little children (Matt 11:25–26).

- He specifically delights in being a Father to the fatherless and an advocate for vulnerable single mothers (Ps 68:5).[43]

The picture given of God as our heavenly Father in *Princess Lost* comes from the following two biblical passages:

I saw heaven standing open, and there before me was a white horse, whose rider is called Faithful and True. With justice he judges and makes war. His eyes are like blazing fire, and on his head are many crowns. He has a name written on him that no one knows but he himself. He is dressed in a robe dipped in blood, and his name is the Word of God. The armies of heaven were following him, riding on white horses and dressed in fine linen, white and clean. Out of his mouth comes a sharp sword with which to strike down the nations. "He will rule them with an iron scepter." He treads the winepress of the fury of the wrath of God Almighty. On his robe and on his thigh he has this name written: KING OF KINGS AND LORD OF LORDS.
REVELATION 19:11–16

The earth is the LORD's, and everything in it, the world, and all who live in it; for he founded it upon the seas and established it upon the waters. Who may ascend the hill of the LORD? Who may stand in his holy place? He who has clean hands and a pure heart, who does not lift up his soul to an idol or swear by what is false. Lift up your heads, O you gates; be lifted up, you ancient doors, that the King of glory may

> *come in. Who is this King of glory? The LORD*
> *strong and mighty; the LORD mighty in battle.*
> PSALMS 24:1–4, 7–8

Most likely, these passages will be frightening to your survivor, at first. Her toxic shame will cause her to hear statements of God's power, judgment and wrath as being *against* her. His demand for "clean hands" may seem to her like further evidence that she is morally dirty and deserves nothing but wrath from a vengeful God. Therefore, much clarification will be needed. Initially, the most important teaching will come *not from what caregivers say about God, but from what they do—how they demonstrate the love of God in action.* When a survivor is ready for overt teaching, several points about these two passages should be highlighted:

- Jesus will return someday as a warrior and judge. He will not return to hurt his children but he will judge and defeat evil abusers, demonic and human, including slave traders who physically and sexually exploit others (Rev 18:13).[44]

- Jesus is a fierce warrior; however, he does not judge and wage war capriciously, but justly. He punishes evil, and he especially punishes those who abuse others. "With justice he judges and makes war" (Rev 19:11).

- Jesus is mighty and holy, yet loving. He will someday spill the blood of his cruel enemies, but he first shed his own blood on the cross for his enemies (Luke 23:24). "He is dressed in a robe dipped in blood" (Rev 19:13).

- Jesus is the mighty Lord of lords who will come to deliver his people (Rev 19:16).

- Unrepentant evil people, no matter how powerful they are on earth and no matter how effectively they escape justice in this life, will eventually face the inescapable judgment of God.

- God is a majestic, glorious King who loves his children (Ps 24:10; cf. Ps 23).

- God loves to forgive humans when they confess their sin. When they do so, he is compassionate and completely forgives (Pss 103:8–17). At the same time, he particularly hates abuse and will not allow unrepentant abusers into his presence. Those who have bloodstained hands and perverse hearts, who refuse to turn from their abuse to pursue justice and mercy, will not stand in his presence (Isa 1:15–18, Ps 24:4).

TRAUMA IS CONTAGIOUS

As a mentor, it is natural to feel overwhelmed as you listen to stories of cruel and inhuman atrocities. It is to be expected that you will feel deeply the effects of profound grief—as if you also are in mourning. You may experience to a lesser degree the same terror, rage, and despair as the survivor.[45] This phenomenon is called *vicarious traumatization*[46]—and includes the entire range of your emotional reaction to the survivor and to the traumatic event itself. As you listen, you may be triggered with your own traumatic history or may notice imagery from the survivor's story that intrudes into your fantasies or dreams.

Just as a survivor needs others to help her heal, you will need others to support you as a caregiver. Just as the survivor needs a community of caregivers around her, so do you. Therefore, your primary task is to create and maintain your own supportive and healthy community. Your personal support community will help you grow, heal in your own ways, and maintain healthy boundaries in the mentoring relationship.

The survivor and her support community will have a directed healing pathway that will be an invitation into additional healing for each individual. This community-based model can be adapted easily by differing communities with differing levels of resources.

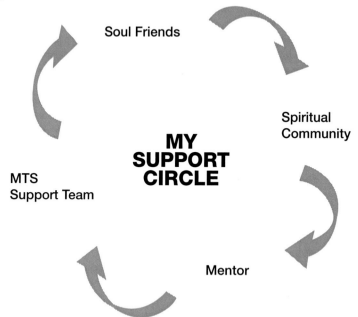

"Clinicians spend 75 percent of their time establishing trust, while peers can start from a place of trust."[47] Someone who has exited successfully and healed from sexual exploitation can convey hope in a way that others cannot. Survivors who have healed provide living examples of the fact that people can survive and experience restoration. When caregivers are equipped and prepared to share parts of their story of abuse and healing, it infuses hope to the survivor who has yet to share any of hers.

INTERACTIVE EXERCISE FOR THE GIRLS: IMAGING LOSS

After reading aloud chapter four of *Princess Lost*, invite the survivor to share her thoughts and feelings. Listen and validate as she shares. If she has not already done so, encourage her to write the names and phone numbers in her journal of two people who feel safe to her. These are people with whom she can share her feelings and thoughts, people who will listen, validate, and affirm. These are people she can call if she feels alone and afraid.

Support her in beginning the process of itemizing the losses she has experienced. She can either record these losses in her journal, or draw, collage, or paint them. As she expressively creates, she is making the invisible, visible. This process is extremely validating of her pain and life experiences. She is integrating her fragmented pain as she grieves (feels and expresses) the loss. Encourage her with the truth of God's power to heal and redeem what she has lost. This is NOT the end of her story!

I have had young girls create songs and/or expressive dance as a part of their grief. They will enjoy expressing/performing this music for you and also enjoy performing it for others. Sometimes they will even want you to join in! There will be pain comingled with laughter and joy. You will make memories together that you will never forget. Sometimes I take pictures of these dramatic "sessions" and then bring one back framed for her room. Remember that you are creating layers of new experiences—safe, nurturing, comforting, loving layers—that will eventually overpower and outnumber the layers of abuse.

CHAPTER 5

⤫

The fright of a Bite

After catching her breath, she realized that she had been hurt—
seriously hurt—and mostly in ways that were hidden.
The bites and scratches had left ugly and thick bands around her heart.
She knew she could not remove these bands, no matter how hard she tried.
They felt rusty, thick, and rough, squeezing out all
the princess feelings she had known. For the first time in her life
she felt dirty, sullied, and oh, so alone.

Princess Lost, *Chapter 5*

In chapter five of *Princess Lost,* we see that Regina's ultimate capture and exploitation by goblins was facilitated by previous traumatic experiences. When she is sexually assaulted by a distant relative, she blindly flees the house, exposing herself to even greater danger. After the attack, she realizes she has been seriously wounded and feels the internal injuries to her heart and soul. Sadly, in her fright, she does not reach out to safe people for help, but instead is impacted instantly by the effects of the abuse. The toxic shame makes her believe she is dirty or bad. Isolation keeps her from seeking safe help and protection. She reasons, "I got myself into this predicament, and I will have to get myself out."

This describes quite specifically some of the primary effects of early childhood abuse and the vices and lies Satan uses to ensnare girls in prostitution.[48] These dynamics are not self-evident to those who have not experienced abuse. In fact, the effects of abuse are confusingly complex and nonintuitive. First, we should note that childhood maltreatment, particularly sexual abuse, plays a major contributing role in child prostitution. In one study of adult female prostitutes, 70 percent of the women said child sexual exploitation was a conscious factor in their "decision" to be a prostitute; 78 percent had been prostituted as juveniles; 60 percent reported being sexually abused as juveniles; a father figure abused two-thirds of those who were sexually abused.[49] Physical and sexual abuse are also primary factors in adolescents running away and becoming homeless.[50] Adolescents who have run away from home and are on the streets are extremely vulnerable emotionally and physically. They are at great risk of resorting to "survival sex" and of being prostituted. Experts tell us that one-third of the American children who run away or are kicked out of their homes engage in sex for food, drugs, or a place to stay.[51]

THE POWERFUL IMPACT OF CHILDHOOD ABUSE

Abuse is unique in the way it destroys people, literally wounding the soul. It is one of the most significant sources of emotional, physical, and relational damage. Recent neurological research has definitively shown that early childhood abuse, neglect, and the witnessing of family violence permanently alters and damages the brain, resulting in a host of long-term individual and social pathologies.

Child maltreatment has been shown to lead to an incredible number of short- and long-term pathologies. For instance, individuals who suffered abuse or neglect during childhood are much more likely in adulthood to experience:[52]

- Somatic disturbances

- Drug and alcohol addiction

- Physical illness

- Depression

- Divorce and unstable relationships

- Violence and other forms of criminal behavior (according to a U.S. Department of Justice study, being abused or neglected as a child increased the likelihood of arrest as a juvenile by 59 percent, arrest as an adult by 28 percent, and arrest for a violent crime by 30 percent)[53]

To understand sexual abuse as a destructive expression of sexuality, we must begin with the divine ideal. Otherwise, we will have a distorted framework for understanding abuse. Human sexuality, all that we are as males and females, as well as sexual intercourse itself, was designed by God for specific and sacred purposes.[54] The creation account in Genesis 1:26–28 makes it clear that human gender flows out of being fashioned in God's image. ("Then God said, 'Let us make man in our image, in our likeness. ... in the image of God he created him; male and female he created them.'")

Since God does not have gender, how does human gender show us God? Theologians tell us that we image God most exquisitely through our capacity for intimate relationships. The language of the creation account describes God using the plural pronouns *us* and *our*, suggesting that he is not a solitary being, but rather *a supreme being in relationship with himself.* Other biblical teaching clarifies the nature of God's relationship with himself as one of perfect love and intimacy.[55]

The creation account confirms that human gender and the sex act are intended to create and express loving, beautiful, relational intimacy. In a perfect garden, Adam was lonely before Eve was created (Gen 2:18–20). She was created as a woman to complement him as an equal (2:18). Through their physical union, they could reproduce life in the image of God (1:28). God's intent that sexuality would create loving intimacy is encapsulated most powerfully at the close of the creation account. When God says, "For this reason, a man will leave his father and mother and be united to his wife, and they will become one flesh. The man and his wife were both naked, and they felt no shame" (Gen 2:24–25).

In summary, God has made us relational beings. Gender gives us the capacity and longing for intimacy with others.

The most intimate and exclusive of all human interactions is to be the marriage relationship, in which intimacy is expressed through sexual union. Scripture repeatedly sanctions sex in marriage as beautiful, holy, and sacred.[56] Because of this, God instituted grave sanctions for sex outside of marriage.[57]

PRIMARY EFFECTS OF CHILDHOOD SEXUAL ABUSE

When we sin or are sinned against sexually, it forms a unique bond that causes damage far beyond anything else we can do with our body (1 Cor 6:18). In short, sexual relations are to be a beautiful, divine gift—an expression of sacrificial, unconditional love. Sex is to be a source of emotional and even physical life. Tragically, sexual abuse distorts all of this so that sex no longer gives life, but destroys life. In abuse, sex no longer expresses selfless love. It takes and destroys instead of giving and completing.

We can list a few of the most significant consequences of sexual abuse. Each greatly increases a victim's vulnerability to additional sexual exploitation:

1. **Shame.** After being sexually assaulted by her relative, Regina felt "dirty and sullied" for the first time. These feelings are the experience of shame. Shame is one of the most powerful and destructive results of sexual abuse (cf. 2 Sam 13:1–20). Ironically, it is the perpetrator who should feel shame, for he/she is the one who is guilty, not the child. Unfortunately, it is impossible, without help, for a child to sort through or understand

these messages of toxic shame. Those shameful emotions become a projection on the child's sense of self.

This is why a young survivor needs help to identify the emotion of shame. Through education and support, she can, in time, release and reject the shame that is not hers to carry, putting it back on her abuser. Shame is so destructive that sexually victimized girls often believe they "deserve" the abuse they receive.[58] This toxic shame from sexual abuse often leads to revictimization and to other destructive behaviors. The survivor may reason that she is a "dirty slut," so she might as well act like one.

2. **Isolation.** Shame creates a deep sense of worthlessness. Shame drives us to hide from others (Gen 3:8). This relational isolation, then, keeps us from the very God-ordained relationships most needed for our healing. Shame-driven isolation increases vulnerability to additional abusers who prey on the alienated and lonely. Three dynamics lead to isolation.[59] (1) Shattered assumptions in a good/safe world. Instead, the survivor feels that the world is unsafe, and that she is powerless to keep herself safe. (2) Shattered assumptions lead to mistrust, which is a consequence of abuse. *Trust is the cornerstone of relational intimacy.* (3) Numbing or emotional constriction eventually cuts the survivor off from all feelings—pain or pleasure. When emotion is constricted to avoid pain, abuse survivors also miss out on love, because relational intimacy is built on emotional connection and risk taking.

3. **Accelerated sexuality.** God did not intend or design children or young adolescents to engage in sexual intimacy.

When children are forced into sexual relations, it often accelerates their sexuality in destructive ways. This is evidenced both biologically and behaviorally. Research with women who were sexually abused as children shows that they become more preoccupied with sex. Abuse also accelerates sexual development (earlier menarche— a girl's first period). It increases the likelihood of consensual sex with peers, and it reduces the age at which the survivor will have her first child.[60] Sexually abused children of both genders engage in more sexual activity than non-abused children their same age.[61] Adolescents and adults who are sexual abuse survivors have significantly elevated rates of promiscuity (larger number of sex partners) and high-risk sexual activity.[62] Sadly, this reflects both the hypersexuality created by abuse (premature sexual knowledge and experience) as well as a trauma reenactment triggered by powerlessness, especially for women.

4. **Depression.** Severe trauma alters the neurological system, including healthy hormone function, so it is not surprising that depression is one of the most common emotional effects of sexual abuse.[63] Some abuse experts assert that depression is the symptom most commonly reported among women who were sexually abused as children.[64] Depression, in turn, often leads to increased isolation. It also creates a vulnerability to self-medication through drugs or alcohol, which in turn makes a victim even more vulnerable to additional exploitation.

5. **Revictimization.** One of the most tragic and undisputed effects of sexual abuse is revictimization. In other words,

a survivor of sexual abuse is far more likely to be abused again.[65] Two out of every three people who are sexually abused will be abused again, research shows.[66] Certain demographic groups are at even higher risk of revictimization. For instance, children or youth sexually victimized in a given year were found to be 6.9 times more likely to be sexually revictimized the following year.[67] This is part of the cascading effect of unhealed sexual abuse.

There are many reasons for such revictimization. Abuse survivors are more likely to numb their pain with drugs and alcohol, which compromises their self-protective capacities and puts them in high-risk environments.[68] Survivors are often filled with shame and self-blame, so they accept unhealthy relationships with abusive partners. Survivors are often emotionally numb and unable to hear and trust their internal danger signals to people or situations that are unsafe.[69] Survivors engage in high-risk behaviors as a means of coping.[70] A survivor's attempts to numb her negative emotions may also be perceived by sexual predators, who sense the survivor is easy prey.[71]

SURVIVING CHILD SEX SLAVERY: A LETTER

The following letter is written by a survivor of childhood abuse and sex slavery. It takes us into that world and, in many ways, describes it better than any professional could:

First and foremost, I want to thank you for reading this book. Your willingness to learn and educate yourself will make a huge impact on the world.

I would like you to do two things for me. One, take what you learn and share it with every church leader, teacher, health care provider, social worker, counselor, mother, father, sister, and brother you know. Two, I would like you to close your eyes for a moment and try to clear your mind of what you have come to know about sexual abuse and human trafficking. Today, I speak to you not as a victim, nor as a survivor, but as a little girl who was murdered (raped) when she was just six. After this first "murder," she endured multiple rapes, years of molestation, being held hostage, getting beaten up, and being shot at.

This is because one day, this little girl played in her room while her mommy went to work. There were no strangers, no kidnappers; she thought she was safe. She was visiting her mommy during a break from school, after her parents split up. She was sad that her parents weren't together, but knew they both loved her. As she played on the floor, the door opened, and her older cousin stepped in and asked her if he could make her lunch. The little girl was excited as can be, jumping at the opportunity, since he was usually so mean and always busy with his friends and out driving around.

He talked sweetly to her and played a few games, then told her about another game they would play. For this game she had to be very quiet. He took her back to the bedroom, he touched her, had her touch him, and eventually ended up raping this six-year-old little girl. The little girl went to the bathroom to wash away the tears and blood. As she rinsed off her face she looked into the mirror and saw me. I still remember the moment she died; it was in that moment that she began to physically change. She was gone for good.

The reason I say she was dead is because her entire future, existence, and soul were forever altered that day. Today I am very proud of the person I am, but I will NEVER know who that girl might have been.

I went back into the room as I was told. Moments later, my uncle walked in to see him fondling me and punished us both by sending me to the corner and explained to us how bad we were for touching each other. There was a ten-year difference between the two of us. He explained to us how WRONG we were, and that he wouldn't tell our moms if we promised never to do it again.

There are several major problems here. The first is that his reaction directly blamed me for the sexual abuse instead of protecting me from the teenage boy who was sexually victimizing me. I experienced deep shame and guilt, believing myself to be the one at fault. Secondly, I knew that I must not tell my mom because I had done something wrong and it must have been my fault. It is clear to me today that his response to my abuse caused just as much damage as the actual abuse. He also did not take me to a safe place and ask me what had just happened. Instead, he made assumptions that were inaccurate. Today, I understand and know that the situation was not handled or dealt with properly at all, and as a result my little mind went wild with sexuality. This was the only incident of sexual abuse perpetrated by that cousin. But this one incident was the gateway that led to all the other abuse I would endure as I grew up.

Finally, when I was nine, I told my mother what had happened. She flipped out and called the police, bursting into hysterics. My mother's reaction did not help me, and neither did sitting in a little cement room and showing five male officers on a teddy bear which holes he put his penis in. Nor did the counselor who had me pretend a pillow was my abuser's face and had me beat it with a bat. I didn't learn a single thing about the effects of sexual abuse on me as a child—help in understanding why I was acting out like I was at that time. I was very sexually precocious and acted out with other kids my age. Today, I know that this sexualized behavior was linked to my original abuse.

There were lots of signs. Once, I was really good in school. Halfway through first grade, I started acting out in class. As a result, I was consistently moved to the back and secluded from the rest of the students. This furthered my isolation and increased my anger. I got violent and told my dad things like, "I hope you die," and "I want you to get hit by a truck," when he would drop me off places. I lit things on fire. I hated school. I made up ridiculous, over-the-top stories to get attention. I lied constantly.

But no one stopped to tell me, "You act this way because you were abused. This is the way you hide your feelings. It is not your fault." The longer I went without healing, the worse the effects became. My mom did the right thing by taking me to a counselor. The problem was that my counselor didn't specialize in sexual abuse and I didn't stay there long enough to build a true healing bond with her.

While I was seeing this counselor my older sister was sexually abusing me. This went on for more than six years. She would do things to me while we were watching movies as a family. I never told, because I was conditioned to think I was wrong and that something was wrong with me. I didn't tell my counselor. I didn't tell my parents. No one ever knew.

Both cases of abuse were RIGHT under my parents' nose. It was not the guy from the alley. I wasn't pulled into a big blue van, and I didn't know how to protect myself because I trusted these people for one, and because I didn't get the help I needed, and because no one saw the signs.

Of course, things got worse. I wanted so badly to fit in and loved ANYONE who showed me affection. My first real boyfriend treated me like crap, and started doing meth. I followed him quite easily when I was sixteen. Why not? I had been numb for the last ten years of my life. I didn't feel anything, and meth made me even more emotionally numb. Eventually, he left me, but not before sleeping with other girls in front of me, calling me names, and making me scream in pain when we had sex. I had NO confidence and not once did I stand up for myself.

I finally got cleaned up. I moved into an independent living home and really started taking some huge steps forward in life. I was working toward my GED, working at a job, and doing great. I was doing good things, and it made me feel good. For the first time, I was surrounded by people who "got" me, and it felt good. However, my inner confidence was still gone, and people could pick up on it. One of the women my mom worked with befriended me, "loved" me, and then sold me to a group of men. This time, I did not fight back at all; I stared at the ground and did everything I was told. I was raped, fed like a dog, forced to sleep with the grossest of men, and couldn't even use the bathroom when I needed to, but had to ask for permission. I slept behind a couch and was no longer even human. I felt like a pet. They never called me by my name; they all spoke a different language. Once again, I was killed, but this time, I was still me. It was just another step on my ladder of life. The three-hour rape, the forced oral sex—I wanted so badly to get high again, but they wouldn't even give me that.

Eventually, they let me go after three months of utter hell. Mind you, this whole time I was blaming myself. I got home and went on a drug binge for months, cleaned up, moved to California and started fresh, got registered for school, got a job, and really started to turn myself around. I was living with extended family who had taken me in to "help" me. One night, I was in the hot tub with my aunt and she forced herself on me sexually. I did not fight back. I did not scream. I didn't tell her to stop. I just sat there, still, and let her do it. Why? Because this was my life! I never once was told that it wasn't my fault, that others were the ones that were sick. I was left wide open for every type of abuse out there because of one man, one incident, and one reaction. Once the damage was done, I basically had "COME RAPE ME" written on my forehead and anyone who noticed took advantage of it.

After this, I left and went on horrible binges, started using needles, lost weight (down to 73 pounds), was up for weeks at a time. I was even read my last rites. I was literally the walking dead. Every time I picked myself up, someone exploited my vulnerabilities, tearing me down until I didn't have the confidence or the strength to stand against them anymore.

Finally, at my worst, I met a wonderful man who told me how beautiful I was, told me I deserved more than what I was given, and told me he would protect me and help me to get better. (He is now my husband.) I had no idea that the effects of abuse were still haunting me until I started my healing. I was so proud just to be out of that part of my life. I haven't looked back since the day I left "the life" almost seven years ago. At that time, I masked everything I went through, picked myself up, and moved on with my life. I gave birth to three amazing babies, joined the PTO, found a love for photography, and settled down to make a wonderful life.

Then, a year ago, somebody said to me, "That was not your fault." That is when I began to really heal! At that time, I began meeting with a mentor from Mending the Soul who began to spend consistent time with me. The first day we met she let me talk and did not judge me. This was very healing for me because I have been judged my whole life. She was accepting and cared about everything

I had to say. I have experienced a lot of spiritual abuse throughout my life. As a result, I was very put off by religion, and was very afraid I would have to "pretend" to be of a certain faith to get the help I knew I needed. I also knew that if I pretended, I would not heal properly, so I was very straightforward with this the first time we met. Honestly, if I felt I was being "preached at" I would have run the other way. There was a point when I really hated God and wanted to know where this God was when I was six and being molested, or where he was during the hours I was being raped when I was seventeen, or how he could let me be so weak. I was still at this point when I met my Mending the Soul mentor.

She accepted me, including my beliefs, and did not judge me. I knew her beliefs but they didn't scare me because she accepted me for who I was and didn't try to change my mind. What scares me is that other girls may not be as "upfront" about their feelings, so there has to be extreme caution when meeting with them and hearing what they have to say. If my mentor would have smiled and nodded but subtly shifted her body or changed position I would have picked up on it and not been able to trust what she was really saying. I actually wanted to meet with her the second time!

There were a few key things that really got the ball rolling. The first helpful thing we did was she began to teach me about the different types of abuse and the effects of these. Then we worked together on my timeline (trauma narrative) so that I could begin to pinpoint the different times I had been abused and then understand my responses to this early abuse. Secondly, she taught me that I wasn't "crazy" by helping me to understand my body and brain's responses to my early trauma as PTSD. I had been told I was bipolar my whole life. Just having this information helped me come to terms with what I had been going through. My mentor has been a trustworthy friend, loving me (and my children) from the beginning. We have become a family and that is why I can share my most intimate, deepest secrets with her. It's her love that has truly made a difference. She is my mentor and is always there when I need her, honest and caring.

When we first began meeting I was having horrific nightmares every night. Insomnia, anxiety, frustration, anger, and my triggers interrupted my thoughts multiple times a day. I couldn't drive within ten miles of any of the places where I was abused.

Today, I am a strong and very confident woman. I have had the strength and courage to do so much, and I am going to change people's lives for the rest of mine. In the year since we've been meeting, my anxiety is much, much less; my nightmares are gone for the most part; my triggers are still there but I am in control now and know what to do when it happens. I have visited all of the places that had such a huge negative impact on my life, and could feel for the first time my feelings about that exploitation. I was strong enough to sit at each one and process my feelings. I cannot adequately tell you how huge that is!

Today I can stand up for myself and say "yes" or "no" in a way that is connected to my feelings. I can do all of this because of the healing that I have experienced. I've also been able to visit churches without the fear in my heart I had previously felt. I truly feel like an unstoppable force and I have set out to change the world around me. In the past twelve months, I have developed confidence and strength that was essentially non-existent before.

So many great things have happened since I began my healing through Mending the Soul. I received a very prestigious scholarship because I had the confidence to go in blazing with no inhibitions. I've been elected president of the Teachers of Tomorrow Club on my college campus. Today, I have the strength to stand in front of people and not feel dirty or ugly. Before, I would not have even joined a small group. There is so much more I could say, but I'm sure you get the point.

It has not been all rainbows and sunshine mind you. It's painful to heal. I've uncovered wounds that I had once deeply buried. I have felt the pain of being a six-year-old baby girl being hurt in the worst possible way, feeling her feelings of anger and fear. I have sat and wept in the parking lot where I was brutally raped for hours, and I felt it. I processed it and I walked away knowing I'm safe. I still have a long way to go, but I have come so far and know I'm going to lead a very happy, fulfilling life. Even though I've endured so much pain I have a lot of love and compassion to now share because of my healing.

One of the biggest things about the *Princess Lost* curricula is the MTS mentor model. I don't know a single person who has gone through a hard time (and I know a lot) who doesn't want to help others the same way they have been helped. I am still being mentored but have begun to help others with the same help I have received. In helping others I am continuing to heal.

A good mentor will love unconditionally, as you would a child. She will be accepting and nurturing, and above all genuine, sincere, and REAL. A victim will pick up on a fake persona and want to expose her. There will be no gaining that trust back and the whole healing process will be brought to a halt. That victim may not want anything to do with healing for a long time. Victims have had their humanity ripped away from them and all they need is to feel loved—real love—and they will do the rest. No one wants to be broken.

Today, I can say with the utmost confidence that I am truly an amazing person, and I know without a doubt that I am going to change lives and mend souls. I would not change a single thing that has happened to me. I will always miss that little girl, but I know that in her place is an amazing person, a loving mommy, a future educator, an artist; for once in my life I am really me. Every lost little girl out there has an amazing woman just waiting to take her place. We need to help them find their way home. The pimps, the child molesters, the rapists are all out there and will continue to destroy. It's a horrible tragedy when a child's soul is ripped away from them, but the quicker we can get to them, the better chance they have at a normal life. I hope that what I have said gives you a better understanding of abuse, and that you will share what you have learned with everyone you know.

The lengthy letter above gives us an invaluable view into the trauma and tragedy of a survivor. As a mentor, your task is to know the nature of trauma and understand how it is internalized in the brain and body of the survivor—how it is felt, perceived, and acted upon. Avoid assuming the depth of impact you would imagine experiencing from the known information you have about the trauma. She is the "expert" on her own experiences (how the abuse has impacted her) and, thus, must be heard, believed, and respected.

Depending on the age of the survivor, these inner connections might be best expressed through projective methods such as: art, movement, dance, clay, and song. Because your survivor might have difficulty finding words for her experiences, the provision of various art media is essential. I like to provide various journal options, sketch pads, chalks, pastels, crayons, watercolors, and brushes.

As your survivor begins to unfold her story, she will be watching you closely to make sure you can handle the "bad stuff." She has been groomed to protect and take care of others at her own expense, so you must demonstrate your ability to handle the traumatic stories she begins to tell. As she trusts you, she will be able to move beyond the reconstruction of the details of what happened to her, to share and feel what she felt at the time of her abuse. As you continue your time together, she will be integrating the fragmented parts of her story and grieving the losses in a safe and comforting relationship.

Help her describe her feelings with the same painstaking detail she gives to facts. As she begins to connect to her feelings, she might become agitated or distant and withdrawn. This is because the trauma is stored in her body and fragmented mentally. She is not just describing what she felt in the past; she is actually reliving it in the present. She needs your support in helping her to modulate the remembering by guiding her back and forth between the trauma of the past and the safety of the present.

Make a list of safe images, people, or objects that she can utilize for support as she needs them. Reassure her that she is not alone in doing this work, that you and others are doing it with her. There is a section in her *Princess Lost Journal* marked "Safety." As she shares her story, you are providing context for her scary and traumatic memories, cognitively, emotionally, and morally.

RECONSTRUCTING HER STORY

"Once upon a time ... "
Reconstructing the trauma narrative begins with the beginning of a survivor's life—her early history before the abuse began. This is an important part of putting the abuse and trauma into its proper perspective and context. Invite her to talk about her early memories, her hopes and dreams, her struggles and conflicts before the abuse began. In a very real way, the trauma has splintered and separated her from the whole of her story. The creation of a timeline will help her connect to her whole story and will be an activity that she will probably be drawn to.

I'll use my experience with one young survivor as a case study in reconstructing your survivor's story. I'll never forget how this survivor first described herself. "I'm just a bad girl. I have anger problems and was a bad influence on my sister. I took her with me the first time I ran." Her false guilt and shame made her feel responsible for the many times she had run away from home. After reconstructing her story it became clear to this young girl that she was running away from home, and taking her little sister with her, because she was trying to protect her. She was running away from abuse. Children don't run away from love. It was painful to hear her falsely attribute the clear and identifiable effects of early childhood abuse to herself. She truly believed it was all her fault.

As we began to construct her timeline, she wanted to talk about the years after she was sold and living on the streets, surviving in whatever way she could. She described the first time she drank to the point of passing out and then the months she had lost to meth. She talked about the numerous times she ran away from home—literally, out to the streets—and the times she tried to come back home. As her trust deepened in me, she began to disclose the early sexual abuse she had experienced. Her stepfather sexually abused her first. Then her uncle, and eventually a live-in boyfriend in her mother's home. As she began to layer these painful events onto her timeline, she made a startling discovery. She was able to identify a pattern that occurred over and over again throughout her childhood. Every time she was sexually abused, she ran, in an attempt to keep herself safe! Reconstructing her story was essential for her to make these crucial connections. As a result, she was able to begin healing and lifting the self-blame she had carried throughout her life. This began to help her understand and heal her shame.

At the age of six she was sexually abused by her stepfather. She tried to tell her mom, but was instead blamed for the abuse and made to apologize to her stepfather. Subsequently, this sexual abuse continued for four years until she ran for the first time, leaving home with her younger sister. This was also the first time that she began to drink to the point of passing out. It was not until she created her timeline that she was able to visualize the cycle of abuse: running, drugs, and eventually sexual slavery. She was empowered by identifying her perpetrators and then connecting her drug and alcohol binges to the first several months of being back on the streets after repeated episodes of sexual abuse.

In one of our meetings, she made the horrifying and shocking discovery that there was not one year in her childhood or adolescence in which she had been protected from sexual abuse. Nor had there been one time when she had been comforted afterward, not until our meeting. This was the first time that she cried during our time together. The unspeakable had been spoken, felt, and expressed, in a context of relational safety and comfort.

Repeated betrayal and trauma fragments the developing sense of self for a young child. As a result, survivors have an arduous task in re-creating their sense of personal identity. Some had "owners" to further control and isolate them. They may have been given false names, fabricated histories, and forged identities. Many girls have been physically branded or tattooed with the name of their pimp or "boyfriend." This serves as a painful and visual daily reminder of the lie that she "belongs" to someone else—that she is not her own.

Isolation further compounds the false guilt and sexual shame these girls carry for their "lifestyle." They have been rejected or abandoned by all healthy relational systems: families, friends, community, school, church, and other social institutions. This extreme relational isolation has fragmented their developing personality. It embeds hideous lies about themselves, others, and God/spiritual authorities into their belief system.

Implications for Mentors

- **Normalize her responses.** Without minimizing her individual pain, assure your survivor that she is not abnormal or crazy. Trafficked girls who have been in the system have probably been given multiple diagnoses, such as borderline personality disorder or bipolar disorder. These labels are often very shameful and discouraging to the girls because they further the self-attribution of labels like "crazy" that they already struggle with. These girls have been labeled, blamed, and verbally violated throughout much of their development. Your gentle education and validation will help your survivor believe that her reactions to the evil atrocities she has experienced are normal and understandable—and that they may diminish in time.

- **Encourage her to name her abusers or perpetrators and to use language and/or art to express her feelings and experiences.** For instance, early in the process of working with a severely abused adolescent girl, I will teach her words and labels for her experiences. We will focus on a particular experience or memory, such as the feelings associated with being exploited. She will then practice describing this feeling until she has her own language for it and clearly understands and connects to how it feels. Then, she will practice attending to that feeling and connecting it with present people and events. In Appendix D you will find two feeling charts, one of words, and one of feeling faces. Use these charts when mentoring, as they will help her to identify and name their often complex emotions. As an example of the empowering victories that result from doing this feeling work, a young survivor who had recently come out of prostitution called me and described being able to set a boundary with a professor who was asking her to do a videotaped interview and tell her story. She told me that for the first time in her life in *real time* she felt the *feeling* of exploitation, and, thus, could for the first time in relationship with a male authority figure, say "no." We celebrated this victory together!

- **Share the emotional burden of the trauma.** The most sacred gift we can offer a survivor is to carry her pain with her. To feel with her, what she feels about her past sexual victimization and exploitation. This will be draining and will require much more from you than a posture of impartial listening. You will be permanently altered by what you hear. Emotionally invested listening is never cheap. As you mentor, remember to attend to your own feelings and needs by establishing and utilizing your own support community.

- **Construct a new interpretation of the traumatic experience that affirms the value and dignity of the survivor.** For example, it is very common for childhood trauma survivors to carry a deep sense of shame about their unworthiness. Some believe they were selected for abuse or exploitation because they were ugly, stupid, or just plain bad. It is helpful for them to understand the bigger picture of their abuse and factors that led to it: a mentally ill parent, an alcoholic father, poverty, or parents who were survivors of their own unhealed childhood abuse. You play an important role as an objective listener and, therefore, can shine truth on her memories.

• **Be validating!** One incest survivor recounts: "Keep encouraging people to talk, even if it's very painful to watch them. It takes a long time to believe. The more I talk about it, the more I have confidence that it happened, and the more I can integrate it. Constant reassurance is very important—anything that keeps me from feeling I was one isolated terrible little girl."[72]

• **Ask thoughtful, specific questions about the impact of the trauma.** Truth telling is empowering and will restore a sense of strength to the survivor. The "action of telling a story in the safety of a protected relationship can actually produce a change in the abnormal processing of the traumatic memory. With this transformation in memory comes relief of many of the major symptoms of post-traumatic stress disorder."[73]

INTERACTIVE EXERCISE FOR THE GIRLS: CREATING A TIMELINE

Creating a timeline helps the survivor anchor to both the truth of her God-given original design and the truth of her history. When the survivor begins to construct this timeline, she gains a sense of mastery over her past and present. This can be very grounding for her and will probably be an exercise that she enjoys.

She can use the pages provided in the *Princess Lost Journal,* or she can create her own timeline in a notebook or sketch pad that you provide for her. Either way, *it is something initiated by her and processed by her, as she is ready.* Ask her how she would like you to support her in this exercise. Provide her with various art supplies such as oil pastels, colored pencils, crayons, magazines, glue, and a sketch pad to encourage creative emotional expression.

Encourage her to record all that she remembers. She can begin with the data: the place and date of her birth, the houses and schools she attended, the people in her family, number of siblings, etc. Encourage her to begin with the most neutral and factual information. As she heals, she will continue to add more painful layers to her story and timeline.

CHAPTER 6

A Kiss

His words dripped like
honey and his voice was
smoother than oil.
He spoke of love and promises
of care. She was hungry
and oh, so thirsty;
how she wanted to believe his words!
A carnival spun in her head.
She wanted to trust him, of course.
She bit her lip—it was dry and parched.
She had never been this desperate before,
nor felt so ugly and plain.
As her mind rushed helter-skelter, she stifled a cry.
Without asking or waiting for an invitation,
he reached into the space that was hers,
his lips scraping over her cheek, and kissed her with
a force that she had not experienced before.
Immediately, she felt the curse.

Princess Lost, *Chapter 6*

A kiss: The signal of his betrayer.
Then all forsook him and fled.
MARK 14:44–50

Perhaps the ultimate example of treachery leading to abuse is found in the Gospel accounts of Judas kissing Jesus. This beautiful Middle Eastern ritual of friendship was perverted into a deceptive, obscene act of betrayal. Judas offered a sign of brotherly affection so that Jesus could be tortured to death. One of the most diabolical realities of child sexual exploitation is the way that pimps and traffickers prey on destitute, vulnerable, and often naive girls. They lure them in with promises and actions that appear to communicate help, friendship, and kindness, only to trap and misuse them. One incarcerated pimp boastfully and succinctly articulates this deceitful betrayal: "With the young girls, you promise them heaven, they'll follow you to hell."[74]

It is often hard for those who have not experienced childhood abuse or neglect to understand how young children and adolescents can naively trust pimps and traffickers and not see through their schemes. We must remember that, in the vast majority of cases, youth who are lured into a life of sexual exploitation have basic unmet needs that heighten their vulnerability. Most often, they have already experienced the deep wounding of early neglect and childhood abuse, providing them with little or no baseline for healthy relationships. We see many of these dynamics in chapter six of *Princess Lost.* Regina is no longer comforted and guided by Whistler's song. She has already experienced hidden wounds from her step-uncle's sexual assault. For the first time in her life, she scoffs at Whistler's words and finds no comfort in thoughts of her Papa King.

There is much irony in the song Regina rejected, "As you are walking." It comes from Scripture and was written by Solomon to guide his own son and to keep him from danger, particularly the danger that comes from immoral or otherwise ungodly individuals. Solomon states:

> *My son, preserve sound judgment*
> *and discernment,*
> *do not let them out of your sight;*
> *they will be life for you, an ornament*
> *to grace your neck.*
> *Then you will go on your way in safety,*
> *and your foot will not stumble;*
> *when you lie down, you will not be afraid;*
> *when you lie down, your sleep will be sweet.*
> *Have no fear of sudden disaster or*
> *of the ruin that overtakes the wicked,*
> *for the LORD will be your confidence*
> *and will keep your foot from being snared.*
> PROVERBS 3:21-26

The healthy person treasures wisdom (Prov 3:13–18) and will prioritize wisdom by humbly obeying and trusting in God (Prov 3:5–7), by avoiding ungodly people (Prov 1:10–19, 2:12–19), by listening to wise people (Prov 2:20, 13:20), and by studying and clinging to God's word (Prov 3:1–2; Ps 119). Unfortunately, Regina's internal wounding numbed any internal sense of danger, for "she had never been this desperate before, nor felt so ugly and plain." It was at this exact point of vulnerability that the handsome goblin emerged, speaking "of love and promises of care."

The description of the deceptive goblin in *Princess Lost* also comes from Proverbs: "For the lips of an adulteress drip honey, and her speech is smoother than oil; but in the end she is bitter as gall, sharp as a double-edged sword. Her feet go down to death; her steps lead straight to the grave" (5:3–5). While this passage is about an immoral, seductive woman and not a pimp, it gives us principles that are specifically applicable to child prostitution. Immoral, ungodly people can be very seductive and appealing, completely blinding their naive victims to the deadly consequences that association with them will bring.

This brief introduction to the betrayal involved in child sexual exploitation gives us much greater compassion and understanding for those ensnared in this evil enterprise. We will now give a fuller explanation of the dynamics involved with entry into child prostitution.

DYNAMICS OF ENTRY INTO JUVENILE FEMALE PROSTITUTION[75]

There are various pathways into juvenile prostitution. Most of these pathways overlap, but differences must be noted. Every individual has his or her own story, life circumstances, and vulnerability factors that contribute to the path they follow. However, specific risk factors have been identified:[76]

- **Lacking attention**–a basic human intimacy need

- **Needing love**–a need to be wanted or to belong to someone

- **Excitement**—a characteristic of healthy adolescent development

- **Money**—needed for survival

- **Drug and alcohol**—dependency/addiction, which is often forced initially

- **Gang affiliation** or abduction by gangs

- **History of early childhood abuse,** particularly sexual abuse

- **Chaotic or dysfunctional family of origin**—these girls don't have family trees, but family bushes

- **Betrayal by significant authority figures in their lives**—stepparents, foster parents, teachers, pastors, coaches, etc.

- **History of running away from home**—when a child frequently runs away from home, he or she is running away from something, such as abuse or lack of protection and/or nurture

- **Homelessness**—pushes them into "survival sex"

- **Low academic performance or school attendance**[77]

- **"No one to help them"**—reported by 98 percent of girls

The picture arising from these findings is a "tangled web of interrelated risks, each producing many serious social and psychological effects, and leaving the individuals involved at the further risk of worsening circumstances."[78]

We make several suggestions based on the research findings:

1. **Include the survivor in her own goal setting and structure of treatment plan.** She needs to feel heard, respected, and empowered in her recovery.

2. **Assess her unique needs—physically, emotionally, and spiritually.** Understand entry into prostitution in light of the vulnerabilities that existed at the time of her exploitation, so that these unmet needs (stemming from her vulnerability) can be addressed in her treatment/growth plan.

3. **Give great care to the relationship between prostituted girls and their families.** Typically, these families are dysfunctional at best and abusive at worst. Develop strategies to screen family members, limit, or completely restrict contact with abusive family members, and to address the deep damage created by growing up in unhealthy and abusive families.

4. **Structure a plan that addresses the needs of non-offending family members** so that the family system(s) around the girl is also assessed, supported, and treated.

DISRUPTED EARLY ATTACHMENTS

A child's healthy emotional development depends on the nurturing and safety provided by her family of origin. Universally, children attach themselves intensely to caregivers for survival.[79] This is a God-given drive that provides for needs that the child is unable to satisfy alone. When the child becomes certain of a "safe and secure base,"[80] (which is created through an attentive, loving, and consistently responsive caregiver) he or she is free to develop and mature emotionally and cognitively through the assimilation and accommodation of new experiences.[81] By "attaching themselves to caregivers, children put themselves in constant touch with a powerful protector. The assurance of a 'safe base' to which children can return after exploring their surroundings promotes self-reliance and autonomy, while instilling a sense of sympathy and helpfulness to others in distress."[82] A securely attached child continues to grow in an intuitive understanding of healthy, interdependent intimate relationships.

Unfortunately, when a child grows up in a chaotic, neglectful, and/or abusive family, she must psychologically adapt, protecting herself from harmful caregivers and abusive circumstances she cannot stop or control. These children, in fear and desperation, attach themselves even more fiercely to their dysfunctional caregivers, often exhibiting extreme obedience and a preoccupation with anticipating or preventing future abandonment. When caregivers are abusive or rejecting, the child is caught in a confusing double bind in which "avoidance of them competes with [her] desire for proximity and care, and in which angry behavior is apt to become prominent."[83]

This helps to explain why children who have disturbed attachments to their primary caregivers (because of multiple separations, chronic neglect, or abuse) develop extreme reactivity patterns, demonstrated in their inability to tolerate anxiety and frustration. These children may seem overly withdrawn, passive, clingy, and dependent. They may have a heightened sense of vulnerability (overly fearful), rely on self-soothing behaviors such as rhythmical activities, and typically have heightened imaginations.[84] It is then easy to understand why these children have lost faith that there is order and continuity in life. Through their early experiences, they have come to believe that they are basically alone.

Helplessness is the belief that one's actions have no bearing on the outcome of one's life. Mental and spiritual health, on the other hand, is premised on the belief that life has intrinsic meaning and that one's choices determine outcomes (healthy control). Both of these truths are stripped from a child who has experienced early abuse or abandonment. Therefore, an abused child and/or adult will attempt to avoid feeling helpless and out of control at any price.

Because God exists in relationship (Father, Son, and Holy Spirit) and we are created in his image as relational beings, disruptions within these early attachments result in disorganized relationships within the child (intrapsychically) and without (interpersonally). When abused adolescents re-experience relationships that are safe, consistent, and nurturing, they are able to eventually build a bridge of connection to their heavenly Father, seeing him as their powerful and loving protector. *It is difficult, then, to overstate the transformative healing power of authority caregivers who use their power to protect, nurture, and love traumatized youth, even when the youth act out in their pain.* Don't be surprised then, when exploited children and adolescents are distrustful, angry, aggressive, resistant, manipulative, addicted, and punishing. They are children in deep mental anguish, children who believe they are alone in a cruel world, in which there is no real love or support.

THE SEPARATION CRY

"Nobody ever listens to me."
"All I need is a family."

A team of mental health professionals through Mending the Soul have met with, assessed, and assisted numerous commercially sexually exploited girls and young women. In one way or another, every one of them has articulated their two most unmet basic needs: to be heard and to belong. Being listened to (responded to and understood) and belonging to a family are fundamentally important to exploited girls because God has made them (and us) relational beings with a deep-seated need to connect with others. As we have already seen, most sexually exploited girls have experienced deeply chaotic and fragmented relationships from childhood, leaving them with deep relational needs and longings. They are terrified of being alone.

John Bowlby and other social scientists have sharpened our understanding of the human need for relationships by developing theories of "attachment."[85] Attachment research reveals that from the earliest stages of infancy, healthy human development is dependent on healthy attachment to caregivers. Broken, disrupted, or insecure attachments inhibit healthy development and can have a negative impact into adulthood. (The good news is that regardless of early unhealthy relationships, "reparative" relationships can be experienced later in life.) Attachment theorists tell us that, while nonhuman primates express attachment mainly through physical contact, human beings predominantly use signaling to maintain adult/infant proximity. The baby's cry induces adults to provide safety, nurturance, and social stimulation. The capacity to reduce anxiety by soothing an infant is the major maternal quality that reinforces the infant's early attraction and attachment.[86] It is interesting to note that attached toddlers play comfortably away from their mothers while toddlers with disorganized attachments cling fearfully to them.

The correlations beg for application here. We have a whole generation of children and youth crying out in pain, essentially without safe mothers, fathers, or families. They are children who have ceased to speak about what they hunger for. We have a second chance to re-parent them in their adolescence, to hear and understand their cries, and to reduce their anxiety by providing safe places of nurturance, social support, and love.

SAFE/LOVING PEOPLE VS. DANGEROUS PEOPLE

"How can I fight for something I've never experienced?"
—FORMER SEX-TRAFFICKED YOUNG WOMAN

Sexually exploited adolescents have little intuitive understanding of healthy, loving, safe people and, instead, have become habituated to dangerous relationships. They need assistance in understanding the difference. The following comparisons lays out the character differences that distinguish safe people from those who are unsafe. At the proper time, this resource can serve as a helpful teaching tool for the psycho-education of exploited girls.

1. DANGEROUS TRAIT

Extremely possessive, jealous, and controlling.

Dangerous and abusive people are extremely insecure about themselves and their intimate relationships. This is reflected in constantly questioning their partner's loyalty, often being hurt that their partner isn't more committed to them, and questioning or accusing their partner of affairs or having other boyfriends or girlfriends. They often scrutinize whom their girlfriend/spouse spends time with, calling multiple times a day to check up on what she is doing. They seek to control virtually every aspect of the other's life. They do not allow their intimate partners to have their own views, their own lives, their own schedules, or their own possessions.

1. SAFE TRAIT

Personal stability is reflected in trust; gives you freedom to be who God created you to be.

Safe, healthy people find their security in Christ. While they desire intimate relationships with others, they look to Christ, not others, to meet their deepest needs. Thus, they are freed to love others and trust God for their relationships with others. Without being gullible or overlooking real problems, they look for and stimulate the best in others because they trust God to work in the relationship and in the other person. They give others freedom to be who God made them to be and do not seek to control others. They live out the following Scriptures, not perfectly, but consistently:

> Love is patient, love is kind. It does not envy. … It always protects, always trusts, always hopes, always perseveres" (1 Cor 13:4, 7).

> The Lord is with me; I will not be afraid. What can man do to me? It is better to take refuge in the Lord than to trust in man [or woman] (Pss 118:6, 8).

> But the Lord is faithful, and he will strengthen and protect you from the evil one. We have confidence in the Lord that you are doing and will continue to do the things we command (2 Thess 3:4–5).

2. DANGEROUS TRAIT

Ridicules your feelings and wishes, insults or degrades you in private and/or in public. May act loving in public but critical and abusive in private.

Often, abusers are charming in public but demeaning and degrading in private. Their domination, control, and sense of superiority are evidenced by the way they constantly reject, ignore, and even ridicule their friends' or partners' feelings and wishes.

2. SAFE TRAIT

Is consistently kind, gentle, and respectful in private as well as in public.

Safe people exhibit Christ-like love through their active commitment to build others up in word and deed. They will use every possible occasion to compliment and encourage others. They respect and are gentle about others' feelings, even if they can't understand them. When they do confront, they will do so gently and humbly for the purpose of helping the other person grow.

Therefore, encourage one another and build one another up, just as in fact you are doing (1 Thess 5:11).

We were gentle among you, like a mother caring for her little children. We loved you so much that we were delighted to share with you not only the Gospel of God but our lives as well, because you had become so dear to us. Surely you remember, brothers, our toil and hardship; we worked night and day in order not to be a burden to anyone while we preached the Gospel of God to you (1 Thess 2:7–9).

Brothers, if someone is caught in a sin, you who are spiritual should restore him gently. But watch yourself, or you also may be tempted (Gal 6:1–2).

If you keep on biting and devouring one another, watch out or you will be destroyed by each other (Gal 5:15).

3. DANGEROUS TRAIT

Isolates you from family and friends; insults and ridicules your family and friends. Goal is to separate you from all healthy support and make you more dependent upon him.

Because of their own deep insecurities, unsafe people/abusers cut their victims off from all other social resources. They accuse others of causing trouble. They may try to pull the victim away from family members by saying the victim is too dependent on her family or that the family is not supportive. They will accuse the victim of having an affair if she has any opposite-sex friendships or even casual relationships. Sometimes abusers will even make the victim quit her job to cut her off from other relationships and to make her more dependent on the abuser. They will often justify isolating their partners from family and friends and demonstrate their own superiority by insulting and ridiculing these individuals.

3. SAFE TRAIT

Encourages you to have other healthy friendships; seeks to love, support, and minister to your family and close friends.

Safe people seek to love and build meaningful relationships with the important people in their lives. They value their partner by valuing the people important to him or her. They realize that they cannot meet all of their partner's needs and therefore, encourage the person to build healthy relationships with others. Knowing that family members have a special role and influence in others' lives, they will invest in her family, seek to understand her family, and, even when they disagree with her family, they will be respectful.

There are six things the LORD hates, seven that are detestable to him: haughty eyes, a lying tongue, hands that shed innocent blood, a heart that devises wicked schemes, feet that are quick to rush into evil, a false witness who pours out lies, and a man who stirs up dissension among brothers (Prov 6:16–19).

Ruth replied, … "Where you go I will go, and where you stay I will stay. Your people will be my people (Ruth 1:16).

4. DANGEROUS TRAIT

Inability or unwillingness to acknowledge personal fault or responsibility.

This is one of the most universal characteristics of abusers. They simply will not take full responsibility for their behavior; it is always someone else's fault. If they are forced to accept some blame, they will apologize by adding "but," and will make others partially responsible. Abusers have an uncanny way of finding unhealthy partners who struggle with low self-esteem and can be easily bullied and shamed into believing that they (the non-abusers) are always the problem. Closely related to this, unsafe and abusive people often evade responsibility for their mistakes, by posturing themselves as the victim: "Everyone mistreats me," "My boss is unfair," or "Nobody ever gives me a fair shake!"

4. SAFE TRAIT

Consistently takes full and complete responsibility for personal behavior without making excuses or blaming others; quickly apologizes to others and confesses sins and mistakes to God.

Safe people repent when they sin and apologize when they make mistakes. They have a keen sense of their own sin and need of God's grace. You do not have to argue with safe, healthy people to get them to accept responsibility for their behavior. They also exhibit genuine sorrow for the way their sin dishonors God and harms others. Thus, when they do sin against others, they will listen to how their actions hurt and will do all they can to take responsibility and make amends.

For I know my transgressions, and my sin is ever before me. Against you, you only, have I sinned, and done what is evil in your sight, so that you are proved right when you speak and justified when you judge. Surely I was sinful at birth, sinful from the time my mother conceived me. Surely you desire truth in the inner parts (Pss 51:3–6).

On your clothes, men find the lifeblood of the innocent poor, though you did not catch them breaking in. Yet in spite of all this you say, "'I am innocent; he is not angry with me." But I will pass judgment on you because you say, "I have not sinned (Jer 2:34–35).

5. DANGEROUS TRAIT

Rigid, patriarchal model of gender roles; assertions or attitudes of male superiority.

Abusive men often have a very firm and extremely narrow understanding of male/female roles. They often place extreme emphasis on male headship and on women and children being submissive. They distort and ignore much biblical teaching that does not fit their idea of male superiority. Females are often viewed and treated as inferior to males. Thus, female opinions and feelings can be readily discounted. Unsafe and abusive men often believe that they must make their girlfriends, wives, and children completely submit to them, even if they have to use threats or physical force to do so.

5. SAFE TRAIT

Deep and genuine respect for women, valuing women and being willing to learn from them; consistent use of one's masculinity (power, position, etc.) to sacrificially serve others, not to get one's own way.

Safe, godly men see their male role not in terms of power (being the boss who gets his way), but in terms of responsibility to sacrificially serve others. Thus, they put the needs of their friends and family first. Scripture calls men to be loving servant leaders. Safe, godly men are comfortable with women. They value them, and treat them as equals. They prioritize protecting and empowering women and find no humor in chauvinistic jokes or putdowns of women. They ask for women's opinions, take them seriously, and truly believe that God did a wonderful work when he made the female gender.

> *Husbands, love your wives, just as Christ loved the church and gave himself up for her to make her holy, cleansing her by the washing with water through the word, and to present her to himself as a radiant church, without stain or wrinkle or other blemish, but holy and blameless. In this same way husbands ought to love their wives as their own bodies. He who loves his wife loves himself. After all, no one ever hated his own body, but he feeds and cares for it, just as Christ does the church (Eph 5:25–29).*

6. DANGEROUS TRAIT

Unpredictable, extreme mood changes; others never really know what is going on inside this person.

Some have described this as a Dr. Jekyll-and-Mr. Hyde pattern that is very confusing and will often make partners of unsafe people doubt their own judgment. The unsafe person can be very sweet one minute but explode the next. Abusers' bad moods are unpredictable, causing girlfriends/boyfriends or family members to "walk on eggshells" so that they do not set them off.

6. SAFE TRAIT

Emotional stability, patience, honesty about one's inner feelings and struggles.

Safe, healthy people are stable and do not fly into explosive rages. When they do get angry or critical, they will own their anger and apologize. They are generally predictable because they are honest with themselves, God, and others about their inner needs and struggles. They do not hide their inner life and are willing to ask for help; thus, they do not build up explosive, damaging anger. They are willing to confess their sin to others and ask for prayer when they are weak, sinful, or frustrated. Because they are honest and are dealing with their own struggles through prayer and confession, others can also be honest around them. No one needs to walk on eggshells to keep them happy.

> Get rid of all bitterness, rage, and anger, brawling and slander, along with every form of malice. Be kind and compassionate to one another, forgiving each other, just as in Christ God forgave you (Eph 4:31).

> But the fruit of the Spirit is love, joy, peace, patience, kindness, goodness, faithfulness, gentleness, and self-control (Gal 5:22).

> A fool gives full vent to his anger, but a wise man keeps himself under control (Prov 29:11).

INTERACTIVE EXERCISE FOR THE GIRLS: DANGER ZONE!

After reading chapter six of *Princess Lost,* invite your survivor to share her thoughts and feelings. Listen and validate as she shares. Offer focused attention and listen beneath her words. What is she communicating nonverbally that offers clues about her feelings?

Review the list of risk and vulnerability factors with the survivor. Help her to identify the factors she has experienced. Then, guide her in developing a list of needs (how others might be able to support her specifically) and goals (the things she would like to work on changing). As she is supported in meeting these basic needs in healthy ways, it will reduce her vulnerability to men and/or women who manipulate with words so that they can exploit her.

Review the safe/unsafe person chart. Encourage your survivor to pick a safe person whom she has known (or knows) and come up with a relational example for each of the characteristics. Do the same for an unsafe person. These can be shared in a group setting or one-on-one in a mentoring relationship. She might want to dramatize these examples or role-play with you.

CHAPTER 7

The Curse

How could Regina explain the paralyzing effect of the curse
and the power of that hideous black magic?
This remains the most difficult part of her story for others
to understand and believe. I myself think it is the cleverness of
the black magic to deaden the inner, hidden soul of a child
while keeping her body intact. You see, if people can't see the damage,
it is much easier for them to believe it doesn't exist!

Princess Lost, *Chapter 7*

> If I had to describe myself in one sentence, I'd
> say, "I'm a whore." … I think if I hadn't mar-
> ried Brian, I'd be a prostitute. AIDS fazes me
> a bit, but having sex with many men doesn't
> faze me in the least. I am very good at sex, so
> why should it go to waste? I might as well give
> it to as many men as possible. Being good in
> bed has always been my identity because that's
> what I've known for longer than I've known
> anything else. I've been trained to be a whore.
> I know all the tricks of the trade. When I say
> this to my husband he gets very uncomfortable
> and unhappy. He doesn't like to think about
> me screwing at four years old. I feel like I was
> born for it. … I'm even scared of being free
> of the abuse. I have hung on to the damage
> because I'm used to it. It's like being given a
> broken vase. You know what it looks like when
> it's cracked. What will it look like when it's
> fixed? Will it ever be okay or will they put it
> back together skew[ed]?[87]
>
> —SOUTH AFRICAN WOMAN, MOLESTED FROM
> AGES FOUR TO TWELVE BY HER GRANDFATHER

Virtually all people at one time or another struggle with self-
doubt, shame, and self-worth. Many of the most gifted and
accomplished have these struggles. We live, after all, in a
fallen world. Every human being on planet Earth suffers the
effects of the curse. But some, particularly those who have
experienced chronic abuse and exploitation, are engulfed
with these negative feelings. These destructive feelings and
beliefs define who they are. They have never known anything

else. Sadly, they believe they are nothing more than whores. It is, they believe, what they were created for.

In chapter seven of *Princess Lost*, Regina's life takes a most dramatic turn when she finds herself in a dismal cave, her innocence stolen by goblins. The seductive goblin's kiss quickly, inexorably led her into a dark, narrow cavern. Her unexpected new "life" completely transformed her existence, overshadowing and eclipsing her previous life and everything she had found sure.

Her life in a cave threatened not just her flesh, but her soul. Worse than the dirt, mud, and injuries was her sense of "badness," which made her tell her grandmother, "If you really knew me, the places that I have been and the things that I have done, you wouldn't call me your granddaughter." This invisible "soul stain" of shame kept her from leaving the cave. Those who have not known the horrors of cave life would never really understand this one of the many invisible chains that kept her from leaving the evil goblins and their dreadful cave.

A BIBLICAL UNDERSTANDING OF SHAME

> Bring me a long, warm coat.
> You must be freezing.
> No, just ashamed.[88]
>
> —CALVIN MILLER

Scripture has much to say about shame that helps us understand its nature, destructiveness, and prevalence. The English word *shame* and closely related terms appear more than 300 times in the English Bible. By far the most frequent usage of *shame* in Scripture involves the painful mental and emotional experience of "contempt, derision, and humiliation."[89] Shame is arguably the most powerful negative human emotion. It is not inherently unhealthy or destructive, though it very often is, particularly for abuse survivors. Shame results from an inner sense that we have fallen short, that we have failed to be what we should be. The key to understanding whether shame is healthy or unhealthy (toxic) is to determine whether it is grounded in truth about one's behavior, one's guilt, and God's response. For the person riddled with shame, making truth distinctions is exceedingly difficult, if not impossible, without assistance.

Healthy shame is based on truth about God (he is holy and forgiving), about my behavior (I have committed behaviors that God clearly defines as sin), and about the remedy (no matter what I have done, God can and will forgive and restore if I turn to him and confess my sin). Healthy shame works through our God-given conscience (Rom 2:14–15), giving us a painful inner sense that we are guilty of violating the law of God and need to be forgiven. Thus, healthy shame is a divine gift because it can bring corrective hope and restoration through divine forgiveness (2 Thess 3:14).

Toxic shame, on the other hand, is a painful inner sense that I am irredeemably defective, disgusting, and worthless. It is based on multiple distortions about God (he hates me and doesn't love me), distortions about my "sin" (I am guilty of the abuse and thus, responsible for my abuse), and distortions about the remedy for shame (I'm a worthless piece of garbage and can never be forgiven or redeemed). Thus, toxic shame drives us away from God and strips us of all hope. It leaves us with no redemptive options, so all we can do is hide from others, hoping they do not see how disgusting we really are. The result is often to give up and live the type of degrading life that a disgusting person might as well live. Toxic shame often drives survivors of sexual abuse to live the destructive life they have come to believe they were born for.

Effectively mentoring a survivor requires a solid understanding of toxic shame and its relationship to healthy shame. Lewis Smedes' insights are helpful:

> [Unhealthy] shame is like a signal from a drunken signalman who warns of a train that is not coming. The pain of this shame is not a signal of something wrong in us that needs to be made right. Our shame is what is wrong with us. It is a false shame because the feeling has no basis in reality. ... It is a shame we do not deserve because we are not as bad as our feelings tell us we are. Undeserved shame is a good gift gone bad.[90]

Shame and Sexual Abuse

Sexual abuse survivors experience the strongest, most destructive toxic shame. The shame they carry actually belongs with their abusers, but it is an inevitable and twisted consequence that the survivor actually carries the shame. We should briefly note why sexual abuse creates such high levels of shame:

1. **God made our sexuality, particularly our genitals, very sensitive and personal and, thus, susceptible to creating great shame.** The ancient Jews understood this, for some of the Hebrew words for shame refer to the genitals. Our genitals are not shameful, but are so intimate that any

inappropriate exposure or contact can bring overwhelming levels of shame, regardless of whether or not we chose to expose or bodies or consented to sexual contact. Note, for instance, how Tamar, when she was forcibly raped by her brother, experienced overwhelming shame, which she took to her grave (2 Sam 13:19–20).

2. **Abusers transfer their shame to their victims.** God has given all humans a conscience that convicts us when we do wrong. The solution for a painful conscience when we have sinned is to repent. Abusers and exploiters must do something to deal with their intense shame, so, if they do not repent, they will most likely try to transfer their shame onto their victims by shaming and blaming them. Tamar's rapist exemplifies this behavior. After Amnon raped his sister Tamar, he hated her intensely—even more intensely than he had lusted after her. He demeaningly referred to her as "this woman" and had a lowly servant throw her, the royal princess, out the door (2 Sam 13:15–17). Pimps and johns are particularly infamous for their contempt of women in general and prostituted women in particular. Virtually all sexual-exploitation survivors have experienced the most shameful and shame-inducing treatment imaginable from pimps and johns, including extreme insults, sexual degradation, public humiliation, and daily verbal assaults and insults. For the survivor who already feels great shame from the sexual abuse itself, degrading treatment and condemning words amplify her toxic shame.

3. **Abuse and exploitation create tremendous soul damage that often leads to shameful behavior, some of which**

is, in fact, sinful. Those who are sexually exploited often engage in destructive, morally inappropriate behaviors such as drug abuse, sexual solicitation, betraying others to traffickers, and physically assaulting others. The dynamics involved here are complex in terms of discerning what actions are nonsinful survival instincts forced upon children and what behaviors are sinful and, hence, should bring healthy shame.[91] Only God, who alone can accurately see and assess the motives, thoughts, and volition of the heart (1 Sam 16:7, 1 Cor 4:3–5), can sort this out. What we do know is that sexually exploited children are at incredibly high risk of engaging in behaviors that are intrinsically shameful and sometimes sinful. These behaviors in turn intensify the cloud of shame surrounding a survivor.

Spiritual and Psychological Impact of Sexual Shame

Shame is arguably the most destructive psychological effect of sexual abuse and exploitation, for it creates many cognitive distortions. It poisons the well of healing, and greatly intensifies the damage of psychological and spiritual abuse. Toxic shame keeps people frozen in their destructive condition by driving them away from intimacy with God and others. This is most tragic, for these relationships are the very means by which healing takes place. Research has shown that the level of shame directly predicts the degree of damage caused by a sexual abuse trauma.[92]

The more shame the sexual abuse survivor feels, the more damaging the effects of the abuse will be. In fact, one study found that shame, more than the severity of the sexual abuse, most accounted for positive or negative adjustment one year after the abuse had ended.[93] Shame and a reduced sense of self resulting from sexual abuse also lead to other harmful effects, especially in relationships. For instance, a person with a fragile sense of self-identity and a low sense of self-potency (they feel they are merely victims of their circumstances and can do little to effect change) often ends up in destructive relationships and is at much higher risk for being victimized again. Spiritually, this person has a very hard time accepting the love of God and finding a sense of confidence and worth in Christ.

God uses people, like you and other mentors, to patiently and boldly love these survivors. These healthy relationships are critically important in order for survivors to recover from abuse and exploitation.

We are convinced that the most essential quality for professionals and mentors of sexually exploited children is a deep personal experience of the love of God. This involves a seasoned, deep confidence in the power of God's love to redeem broken lives (Rom 5:17–21). By seasoned and deep, we mean a mature, unshakable confidence in the power of God's love that comes from much prayer, wrestling with God over the brokenness of the world, and pursuit of Christ. This will help to mitigate the anxiety that hearing abuse stories can create in us.

The effective mentor must have a strong, growing experience of God's love in the face of his or her own sin. This will give us confidence to keep loving and believing in sexually wounded girls, even when their own shame would tempt us to feel false shame ourselves. A grounded personal belief in God's love will anchor us when hurting survivors displace their anger onto us, or when, in their pain and frustration, they blame us (implicitly or explicitly) for not being a better counselor or mentor, for not being able to fix them faster.

In these times, our confidence and security come from God himself, the one who loves us and delights in us despite our sin. This, in turn, will allow us to let go of our own defensiveness and self-pity, so that we can love fragile and prickly survivors with the boldness and tenacity that healing requires. The effective mentor must have a deep confidence in God's loving redemption in his or her life. God's ability to redeem us assures us that he can also redeem others (1 Tim 1:14, 16).

THE DAMAGED SELF: A BODY DEFILED

For a child, the development of a positive sense of self depends upon a parent's gentle and never-dangerous use of power. A good parent (who is much more powerful than the child) shows regard and respect for the child's individuality and dignity, which in turn creates a sense of value and self-respect within the child. The child also develops autonomy, a sense of feeling separate from, but at the same time connected to, parents. Additionally, the developing child learns to control and regulate her own bodily functions and to form and express her own feelings and opinions.[94] Sexual abuse and trauma disrupt this maturation process in the most fundamental ways.

In sexual trauma and exploitation, the body is invaded, injured, and defiled repeatedly. One of the most humiliating aspects of trauma is the loss of control over one's own bodily functions. At the moment of the first rape, there is a severing of autonomy. The child/adolescent is no longer separate within a relationship. "Shame is a response to helplessness, the violation of bodily integrity, and the indignity suffered in the eyes of another person."[95] To further illustrate, Judith Herman quotes a combat veteran describing the effects of trauma upon a person's ability to trust themselves or others:

> War [violence] has the feel—the spiritual texture—of a great ghostly fog, thick and permanent. There is no clarity. Everything swirls. The old rules are no longer binding, the old truths no longer true. Right spills over into wrong. Order blends into chaos, love into hate, ugliness into beauty, law into anarchy, civility into savagery. The vapors suck you in. You can't tell where you are, or why you're there, and the only certainty is overwhelming ambiguity. ... You lose your sense of the definite, hence your sense of truth itself, and therefore it's safe to say that in a true war story nothing is ever absolutely true.[96]

In rape, whether childhood sexual abuse, adolescent sexual assault, or sexual slavery, it is the victim, not the perpetrator, who carries the guilt.[97] This guilt is often extreme, taking the form of survival guilt. This is the victim's guilt for the very thing she was empowered to do: survive. This is compounded for the adolescent who witnesses the suffering or death of others. She has survived and feels a deep burden of conscience that she was not able to save others, or, worse, that her actions contributed to the endangerment or death of others. The trauma of sexual exploitation takes on added force when violent injury or death is the result of the victim's active participation. It is not just the exposure to death, but, rather, the participation in meaningless acts of malicious destruction that render the victims most vulnerable to lasting psychological damage.

A survivor desperately needs to feel relationally connected (and thus, not alone) while she is supported in talking about her experiences. She needs permission and gentle guidance to label the evil perpetrated against her as abuse and rape, to name the perpetrators if she can. Tragically, conventional social attitudes often fail to recognize prostituted children as victims of repeated rapes, instead believing these children to be having consensual sexual relations for which the child victim is responsible. This collective denial of her sexual victimization abandons her a second time. Not only is she violated by her perpetrators, but she is also abandoned by the communities around her. Therefore, your validation and emotional presence—remaining close and connected to her as she shares the horrific stories of exploitation—is the most healing gift you can offer.

BETRAYAL BONDS AND REENACTMENT: "WHY DOESN'T SHE JUST LEAVE?"

Why doesn't she just leave? The simple answer is that she cannot— not without help. Johns Hopkins researcher John Money commented on child victims who continued to put themselves in harm's way. He observed that the "abused has become addicted to abuse: the response to abuse is to stimulate more of it."[98] This is a shocking statement and one that is difficult to understand. Psychologist Patrick Carnes explains several realities about these dangerous bonds. Understanding these realities helps us to better understand our survivors.[99]

1. Betrayal bonds occur when there exist multiple

layers of betrayal by trusted people the victim depended upon. Bessel van der Kolk has done groundbreaking research on the role of the body's endogenous opioid system (naturally occurring, "opium-like" chemicals in the brain that give a sense of well-being and euphoria) to explain the confusing occurrence of a victim's addiction to trauma itself and to the abuser. He describes the chemical component of this phenomenon as follows:

> Trauma victims continue to re-create the trauma in some form for themselves, or for others. ... [Incest] victims may become prostitutes, victims of child physical abuse may provoke subsequent abuse in foster families, victims of child abuse may grow up to become self-mutilators. Still others re-create the trauma by identifying with the aggressor, and perpetuating the same acts on others that were once exercised upon them. ... [What] these people have in common is a vague sense of apprehension, emptiness, boredom, and anxiety when not involved in activities reminiscent of the trauma.[100]

Endogenous opioid release by the body could also "account for the sense of calm on re-exposure to stress that is reported by many traumatized individuals ... [who] re-expose themselves voluntarily to situations reminiscent of the trauma."[101]

2. **Betrayal bonds can form a life pattern.** Research shows that once you form a trauma bond you are at increased risk and more susceptible to falling into similar rela-

tionships. The very nature of sexual exploitation is the repeated physical and sexual victimization by the one(s) upon whom the victim is depending for survival. Promises of love and care are quickly broken once the victim's dependency is in place.

3. **Betrayal bonds are mysteriously durable.** When a captor creates the right chemistry, by alternating bursts of "loving care" with violence, threats, and degrading behavior, a fierce loyalty and cooperation forms in the victim. This explains the confusing behavior of some prostituted girls who, once rescued, exhibit fierce rage and contempt for those who rescue them. These trauma bonds may take minutes to form, but they are robustly durable, lasting years and at times, decades.

4. **Betrayal bonds can happen to anyone.** You can be from an affluent family, strong, gifted, and educated, but in the context of violence and terror become traumatically bonded. Those who come from painful, dysfunctional families are at even greater risk of trauma bonding. It is not uncommon for prostituted adolescents, after their rescue and recovery from a commercial sexual exploitation ring, to "find" their pimp shortly after they are released. This can be one of the most disheartening effects of trauma.

5. **Betrayal bonds are about survival.** Our drive and ability to connect to each other explains in part how we are able to survive atrocities. We experience psychic terror in relational separation. Therefore, physical danger and threat actually deepen attachment.[102] This trauma bonding is destructive for the adolescent, to

the degree that it results in exploitation and the loss of control over one's own choices—in short, when it becomes addictive.

UNCOVERING HER ORIGINAL DESIGN

> If you have anything really valuable to contribute to the world it will come through the expression of your own personality, that single spark of divinity that sets you off and makes you different from every other living creature.
> —BRUCE BARTON

Buried beneath the toxic shame, false guilt, and betrayal bonds created by sexual abuse rests your survivor's original design, created by her Father God. She is created to reflect a unique set of characteristics found in God himself. It is important to remember that her original design is protected despite the most hideous levels of abuse and trauma. However, tragically, when a child is abused, her perception of herself is shaped, not by her original God-like design, but by the shame and false guilt that she experiences as a result of her sexual trauma and exploitation.

Helping a young survivor uncover her original design and believe the truth of her created beauty and uniqueness can be a daunting task. This is because of the myriad effects of abuse. Because the child's trauma is stored in her body and brain, even after she is physically safe, she will continue to re-experience the abuse. Her body and brain have recorded the trauma and replay it in a way that causes the child, by no choice of her own, to relive the abuse as if it is reoccurring. This is, in essence, the nature of post-traumatic stress disorder. The young survivor struggles to believe that she is safe or that her pimp will not be able to find her again. "The perpetrator does not have to find the child, because the child's brain has recorded the voice, the smell, and the feel of the perpetrator. These sensory experiences are some of the brain's most vivid recollections from the past."[103]

As a mentor, you can help your survivor mediate the above symptoms by supporting her in creating and anchoring to soothing thoughts, images, and people that are safe for her. Once you have created safe anchors together, support her in integrating the intrusive past images and memories into the present. Guide her in remembering and connecting to safe imagery and people from her pre-trauma history. This will help her to put the trauma she has experienced into a proper context so that she can remember and connect to the girl she was before the abuse began. As a result of the abuse and exploitation she has experienced, her identity has been stripped. She must now build a new sense of self, based on her original design. It is at this point that recovery becomes hopeful and encouraging to both of you, because this new image must come initially from people outside of her post-traumatized brain—and that is you!

Take every opportunity you can find, to reflect back to her your observations of her natural gifts, strengths, and temperament traits that you most delight in. She needs daily affirmations and specific, positive feedback in order to see herself in this new positive image. In time, she will begin to perceive herself in the same positive light that you view her in. This is an important part of her rediscovery of herself, as the beautiful girl God originally created her to be.

INTERACTIVE EXERCISE FOR THE GIRLS:
THE REAL ME!

After reading chapter seven in *Princess Lost,* complete the following exercise together. Using a journal or large sketch-pad, draw, collage, or describe in words the answers to the following questions. Encourage creativity by spreading out old magazines, pictures, and newspapers on the center of the table. Offer an assortment of pens, paints, and scissors. Read each question and encourage her to answer it for herself. Then offer your positive observations about her personality, strengths, etc., for her to incorporate into her collage. Be as creative with this exercise as you can.

- What are my strengths?

- What do I most love doing? Not doing?

- What are my dreams?

- What are my goals?

- What skills would I like to learn?

- What are my favorite colors?

- What music makes me want to dance? Favorite song? Why?

- What is my favorite kind of day?

- What is my favorite word?

- What are my favorite foods?

CHAPTER 8

∽

The Lost Years

She felt empty and gutted, a shadow
of her former self in a godforsaken land.
Broken wings, torn dress, colorless, bruised, and scarred;
she dropped her head upon her knees and cried herself to sleep.

Princess Lost, *Chapter 8*

> Have compassion for everyone you meet, even
> if they don't want it. What appears bad man-
> ners, an ill temper or cynicism is always a sign
> of things no ears have heard, no eyes have
> seen. You do not know what wars are going on
> down there where the spirit meets the bone.
> —MILLER WILLIAMS

The princess was now lost, alone, and completely invisible
to the citizens of her Papa's kingdom. She was on the brink
of death and yet unable to save herself because of the power of
the black magic. The effects of abuse and sexual exploitation
isolated, shamed, disempowered, and emotionally numbed
the princess. The goblins forced her dependency on drugs to
further control and disempower her. They were giddy with sat-
isfaction over the paralyzing effects of her condition and the
ways in which she was dependent upon them. Her emotionally
numbed heart cut her off from the previous loving relationship she had enjoyed with her Papa King and even Whistler.
She distrusts both of them now, and their words.

The Scriptures sung by Whistler of Papa King throughout
this chapter are from the Psalms.

> *You are my hiding place and my shield;*
> *I hope in your word.*
> *Depart from me, you evildoers,*
> *That I may keep the commandments of my God.*
> *Uphold me according to your promise,*
> *That I may live,*
> *And let me not be put to shame in my hope!*
> *Hold me up that I might be safe ...*
> PSALM 119:114–117

I lift up my eyes to the hills,
From where does my help come?
My help comes from the Lord,
Who made heaven and earth.
He will not let your foot be moved;
He who keeps you will not slumber.
Behold, he who keeps Israel
Will neither slumber nor sleep.
The Lord is your keeper;
The Lord is your shade on your right hand.
The sun shall not strike you by day,
Nor the moon by night.
The Lord will keep you from all evil;
He will keep your life.
The Lord will keep your going out and your
coming in
From this time forth and forevermore.
PSALM 121

O Lord, you have searched me and known me!
You know when I sit down and when I rise up;
You discern my thoughts from afar.
You search out my path and my lying down
and are acquainted with all my ways ...
You hem me in, behind and before;
And lay your hand upon me.
Such knowledge is too wonderful for me;
It is high; I cannot attain it.
Where shall I go from your Spirit;
Or where shall I flee from your presence?
If I ascend to heaven, you are there!
If I make my bed in Sheol, you are there!

*If I take the wings of the morning and dwell
in the uttermost parts of the sea,
Even there your hand shall lead me,
And your right hand shall hold me.
If I say, 'Surely the darkness shall cover me,
And the light about me be night,'
Even the darkness is not dark to you;
The night is bright as the day,
For darkness is as light with you.
For you formed my inward parts;
You knitted me together in my mother's womb.
I praise you, for I am fearfully and
wonderfully made.
Wonderful are your works;
My soul knows it very well.
My frame was not hidden from you,
When I was being made in secret,
Intricately woven in the depths of the earth.
Your eyes saw my unformed substance;
In your book were written, every one of them,
The days that were formed for me,
When as yet there was none of them.
How precious to me are your thoughts, O God!
How vast is the sum of them!
If I would count them, they are more
than the sand.
I awake, and I am still with you.*

PSALMS 139:1-18

CHARACTERISTICS AND IMPACT
OF "THE LIFE"

To characterize the experience and impact of being prostituted, we must remind ourselves of its brutal, bare essence. Nobody explains this better than Andrea Dworkin, a militant feminist who, after fleeing an abusive husband, was herself forced into prostitution as a homeless young woman. Her essay "Prostitution and Male Supremacy" was originally part of a speech she gave at the University of Michigan Law School, challenging academics to recognize the true nature of prostitution.

> Prostitution: What is it? It is the use of a woman's body for sex by a man; he pays money, he does what he wants. The minute you move away from what it really is, you move away from prostitution into the world of ideas. You will feel better; you will have a better time; it is more fun; there is plenty to discuss, but you will be discussing ideas, not prostitution. Prostitution is not an idea. It is the mouth, the vagina, the rectum, penetrated usually by a penis, sometimes hands, sometimes objects, by one man and then another and then another and then another and then another. That's what it is.

> Prostitution in and of itself is an abuse of a woman's body. Those of us who say this are accused of being simple-minded. But prostitution is very simple. And if you are not

simple-minded, you will never understand it. … In prostitution, no woman stays whole. It is impossible to use a human body in the way women's bodies are used in prostitution and to have a whole human being at the end of it, or in the middle of it, or close to the beginning of it. It's impossible. And no woman gets whole again later, after.

Women who have been abused in prostitution have some choices to make. You have seen very brave women here make some very important choices: to use what they know; to try to communicate to you what they know. *But nobody gets whole, because too much is taken away when the invasion is inside you, when the brutality is inside your skin. … The only analogy I can think of concerning prostitution is that it is more like gang rape than it is like anything else.* Oh, you say, gang rape is completely different. An innocent woman is walking down the street and she is taken by surprise. Every woman is that same innocent woman. Every woman is taken by surprise. *In a prostitute's life, she is taken by surprise over and over and over and over and over again. The gang rape is punctuated by a money exchange. That's all. That's the only difference.* But money has a magical quality, doesn't it? You give a woman money and whatever it is that you did to her she wanted, she deserved.

When men use women in prostitution, they are expressing a pure hatred for the female body. It is as purely hateful as anything on this earth ever is or ever has been. It is a contempt so deep, so deep, that a whole human life is reduced to a few sexual orifices, and he can do anything he wants. Do you understand? She is literally nothing. Now, many of us have experiences in which we feel like nothing, or we know that someone considers us to be nothing or less than nothing, worthless, but for a woman in prostitution, *this is the experience of life every day, day in and day out.*

While Dworkin did not understand the redemptive power of Christ to transform and heal, she deeply understood the destructive, demeaning nature of prostitution. To minister to prostituted girls, we must also understand what "The Life" involves and what it does to a woman. It is particularly important to remember that the experiences listed below are what prostituted females can and often do experience every single day that they are in "The Life."

Characteristics and Strategies of Pimps

The wings of demons are as white
as angels' wings
Their halos are as golden bright
They sing as well as angels, too
But only when it's night.[104]

—CALVIN MILLER

Law enforcement officials report that, in most communities, it is virtually unheard of for adolescent females to be involved in prostitution without a pimp. Understanding the characteristics and strategies of pimps is essential for understanding what prostituted adolescents have experienced and how it has impacted them. For a pimp, it is all about money. Young girls and women are simply a commodity to be sold for extremely high profits. Pimps take virtually all the money made by prostituted victims. A well-managed "stable" can earn a pimp hundreds of thousands of tax-free dollars a year. *Ultimately, all pimps use two of the most powerful human emotions, love and fear, to achieve their nefarious ends.* Their techniques at securing new victims are not irrational; nor are they trivial. They are calculated to achieve their desired end: to overpower and control a human life for financial gain.

There are various types of pimps. The vast majority of pimps are violent with "their girls," but some—"gorilla pimps"—rely primarily on raw violence and threats. These pimps will often kidnap or otherwise force girls into prostitution, quickly "breaking them" through severe beatings and torture, gang rapes, denial of food, water, toilet, etc. In a short time, they have them turning tricks on the street. Their primary, and sometimes sole, method for keeping their girls in line is brute force and threat of violence. Most pimps, however, are more psychologically sophisticated than this, customizing their strategy to each girl after sizing up her unique emotional needs and vulnerabilities. Experienced pimps may spend weeks, or months if need be, to make a girl emotionally dependent on them. They do so by separating her from her network of family and friends and convincing her that they will fulfill all her dreams. This type of pimp is known as a "bait and switch" pimp.

Exploitation and Manipulation

In the book *Prostitution & Trafficking in Nevada*, Melissa Farley and two of her colleagues have written one of the best summaries of pimps and their strategies in print.[105] They emphasize that most pimps recruit through a highly calculated courtship, which can be compared to the "love-bombing" techniques used by cults. Once the pimp works his way inside a girl's head, he can begin to exploit her specific weaknesses, break down her defenses, and systematically groom her for selling her body. He may have sex with her and secretly take pictures, later using them as blackmail against her if she does not begin to turn tricks. He may buy her nice clothes and then later tell her she needs to work off her "debt." He may convince her that he has a pressing financial burden and needs her to make some money on the streets to help him out. He may give her drugs and, once she is addicted, force her to "work" to pay off a drug debt. He may threaten to harm her family, especially her younger siblings. After he and his friends repeatedly rape her by performing multiple sex acts with her, he may tell her that she is now a slut, and that no one will want her, so she might as well make some money from sex.

When his strategy works to "turn a girl out," the pimp quickly reinforces his control through psychological and physical violence. Once a girl is working the streets, she is typically given a daily income quota she must bring in—"or else." While she is on the street and out of the pimp's presence, the pimp still has complete control through his "bottom girl" (a girl who is completely under his control and thus will act on his behalf to control and abuse the new girls in order to control them) and through her cell phone. Not only do cell phones give pimps instant verbal access, but, with mobile GPS technology, they can be used for constant physical tracking. Prostituted girls cannot access social services without serious repercussions. They are generally not allowed to turn a buyer down for any reason and often cannot demand a condom. Victims in prostitution provide sexual services not only on the street but also in strip clubs, as call girls, and in pornography. They effectively live in 24/7 sexual victimization.

Control and Powerlessness

One of the most significant and characteristic aspects of "The Life" is being utterly controlled. Melissa Farley describes this well: "[E]very aspect of the prostituted woman's body is under the control of the pimp who manages and handles her. The pimp's total control over women in prostitution includes what she wears, when and where she can sleep, and what and how much she can eat. … even how much air and light she is allowed to have."[106]

Eventually, the pimp receives her total obedience. Techniques pimps use to achieve control include social isolation, sensory deprivation and torture, deliberate exhaustion, and threats to the girl and to her family. Additional tactics include occasional indulgences, posturing as omnipotent, degradation, forced pregnancy, drugging, forced addiction, and capricious rules.

A chilling 2006 study helps explain the sophisticated strategies that pimps use to gain total control. A study of incarcerated Canadian pimps found that more than 36 percent met the criteria for being a psychopath, while almost three-in-four exhibited psychopathic traits. The Psychopathy Checklist[107] lists four correlated traits of a sociopath: (1) interpersonal—

glibness/superficial charm, pathological deception, cunning/ manipulative, (2) affective—lack of remorse or guilt, callous/ lack of empathy, failure to accept responsibility for actions, (3) lifestyle—parasitic lifestyle, impulsivity, irresponsibility, and (4) antisocial—poor behavior controls, juvenile delinquency. In other words, a high percentage of pimps are the most disturbed, cunning type of criminals. They lack a conscience and also lack the ability to feel empathy for another human being.

We can illustrate typical pimp strategies and psychopathy with some quotes from a "how to" guide written by self-professed pimp Mickey Royal. These quotations from *The Pimp Game: Instructional Guide*[108] make the calloused, narcissistic, evil, psychologically astute behaviors of pimps painfully clear.

- "A pimp doesn't believe in dreams; he sells them. A pimp has no friends, only victims" (page 57).

- "A ho to a pimp is worth nothing. She is actually worth everything, but he must make her believe that she is worthless. A pimp buys her soul" (page 52).

- "You have to know everything about your ho. Some hos need physical abuse. Some hos need emotional mistreatment. … [Y]ou have the emotionally destroyed ho who was raped by her father or uncle who you must keep crying" (page 71).

- "A ho is driven by her insecurities. You find out what her insecurities are and use them against her" (page 76).

- "How to knock a bitch and transform her into a ho? It is an intricate process of psychological destruction and emotional construction" (page 18).

- "After being chosen and invited into a ho's world, you begin to pull her away from that which she loves and most importantly, that which loves her. You have to kill her spirit until she feels it's worthless. She'll then give her soul to you in order to receive the love from you that she now needs" (page 59).

- "Humiliation is one of the fastest ways to destroy self-esteem. It truly gets the ball rolling. I had a ho over [at] a partner's house. He and I played dominoes while she was made to strip nude. While standing, still nude, people came and went. She stood still and cried while visitors touched, poked, prodded and even verbally insulted her. I could feel her pain; then I made the pain stop. This process is called "breaking a bitch down" or "knocking" (page 60).

- "The pimp sucks a ho dry and when she can't turn another trick, she becomes a burden. Then it's back to the curb. A ho's longevity depends on her marketability" (page 38).

Humiliation, Degradation, and Inferiority

Dworkin's essay, quoted in the beginning of this chapter, emphasizes the degrading nature of prostitution. Pimps degrade and humiliate in order to break a woman's will, to make her submissive and dependent, and to "break her in." Degrading sex acts such as gang rape, sex with animals, sodomy, etc., are commonly employed by pimps. Buyers often humiliate and degrade as well because of their misogyny, narcissism, and sexual conditioning by pornography. Many men believe that because they are paying for sex they are entitled to perpetrate degrading sex acts. As one buyer callously stated:

> I don't hire prostitutes for the conversation. I pay her to give me what I want and in my book when you pay the money you're the boss. I give orders and she follows them. So if I want anal [sex] or something a bit out of the ordinary, I get it. Otherwise, I'll find someone else. There are plenty of whores in the sewer willing to do what I tell them for cash.[109]

For many buyers, their distorted belief in female inferiority is a significant factor in their use of prostitutes. The clinical director of a treatment center for buyers notes that most of the johns he has seen do not respect women and don't want to. He explains:

> Real sexual relationships are not hard to find. There are plenty of adults ... who are willing to have sex if someone treats them well and asks. But there lies the problem. Some people do not want an equal, sharing relationship. They do not want to be nice. They do not want to ask. They like the power involved in buying a human being who can be made to do almost anything.[110]

Violence

Prostituted females endure an almost unimaginable amount of violence from pimps and buyers. A 2002 study of prostituted adolescent females concluded, "the young women continued to experience violence as prostitutes so commonplace that it almost seemed 'normal.'"[111] Pimps, johns, other prostituted women, intimate partners, and even law enforcement officers chronically victimized them. Violence is common for all prostituted adolescents and adults. A forensic study found that prostituted women are more likely to be murdered than any other set of women ever studied.

A 2005 study of "street" prostituted women found that 71 percent had experienced a violent encounter in the past three months and 17 percent had experienced a violent encounter with a "date" in the previous month.[112] A study of prostituted women in nine countries revealed that while they engaged in prostitution 95 percent of the (Canadian) women reported that they had experienced violent injuries as a direct result of prostitution, and 95 percent of these injuries included head injuries. Of the American women surveyed, 79 percent reported being physically assaulted while being prostituted; 83 percent had been physically threatened with a weapon; and 73 percent had been raped since entering prostitution.[113] The title of one journal article, a quote from a prostituted woman, says it all: "You just give them what they want and pray they don't kill you."[114]

Mental Health Impact

Prostituted women have greatly elevated rates of depression, anxiety, stress disorders, suicide attempts, and full-blown post-traumatic stress disorder (PTSD). The complex mental health problems of prostitution survivors result from the cumulative trauma and extreme stress they have continually experienced over many years, often beginning with childhood abuse. A 2008 study of four of the largest residential programs for prostituted women in America found that, among the residents in these four programs, 91 percent had experienced childhood sexual abuse, 72 percent had run away as adolescents, 73 percent had been incarcerated, 95 percent had suffered violence while in prostitution, 95 percent struggled with chemical addiction, 86 percent had been homeless, and 95 percent suffered from some type of mental illness.[115]

Numerous studies have found that prostituted women have catastrophically high PTSD rates—40 to 70 percent. We can see how astoundingly high these levels are by comparing them with the current estimated PTSD rate for soldiers returning from combat in Iraq and Afghanistan—just below 20 percent.

Physical Health Impact

A study of 278 street-based prostituted women in Miami revealed that 52.9 percent had symptoms of moderate or severe depression, 69 percent had acute traumatic stress symptoms, 19 percent tested positive for HIV, 48 percent tested positive for hepatitis B, and 19 percent tested positive for hepatitis C.[116] Often, prostituted women experience ongoing health problems from violent attacks. Sexually exploited minors also experience malnutrition, sexually transmitted diseases, HIV/AIDS, and physical and psychological complications from abortions.

Drug Use

Illegal drug and alcohol misuse are strongly, even inextricably, linked to prostitution. Some girls begin using drugs and/or alcohol to numb pain in their lives before they enter the world of prostitution. Other prostituted adolescents are forced to use drugs by their pimps, in order to keep them dependent. Regardless of when drug and alcohol misuse begin, the vast majority of prostituted adolescents and adults are dependent on drugs and alcohol. For most prostituted adolescents and young women it is a primary coping mechanism against the shame, emotional pain, and physical, sexual, and verbal abuse that they suffer daily. One study found that, of the prostitutes surveyed, 70 percent used drugs to detach emotionally while turning tricks, 44 percent used substances to cope with fear while turning tricks, and 54 percent indicated that it was necessary to be high to go through turning a trick.[117]

These girls are incredible survivors. They have faced and survived threats and harm that most of us cannot even imagine. That fact alone should generate great respect from those who know them.

IMPLICATIONS FOR MENTORS AND RESTORATIVE PROGRAMS

1. **Seek to identify the specific strategies that your survivor used to cope and survive on the street, based on her own unique personality and gifts.** While many of these strategies were at times maladaptive, they did serve a purpose. Research tells us that many of these "survival skills" have become great strengths. Help your survivor identify these

strengths and coping strategies. Clarify and define the times when those strategies are helpful, and when they are not. You can also offer new skills and strategies to help your survivor cope with ongoing stress and difficulties.

2. **Reflectively consider the characteristics and strategies of pimps, particularly their willingness to use violence, control, and manipulation.** Pimps will do anything they can to disrupt an outreach program and the subsequent recovery of survivors. They want to get "their" girls back. This will most likely include sending "bottom girls" into the program to secretly recruit or threaten girls. Additionally, pimps may find ways to send messages to your survivor or to her family members. They may threaten you or other staff, volunteers, and mentors. These realities must be factored into program policies and procedures as well as safety measures and protocols.

3. **Assessing for drug and alcohol dependency and offering drug treatment as needed are important parts of any outreach program for prostituted adolescents.** The twelve-step model offers many valuable tools, such as HALT!, which helps a girl in recovery pay attention to the times she is hungry, angry, lonely, or tired—as these are the moments when she is most prone to act out.

4. **In light of the extreme domination and control that prostituted girls have known as normal, listening to your survivor and soliciting her opinions are extremely effective in building trust and creating an environment of safety.** You should seek to incorporate your survivor's views into the program as much as possible. This does not mean

the girls run the program. Rather, this reflects a survivor-centered attitude and communicates deep respect.

5. **Given the extent to which the girls have been manipulated and exploited, volunteers and staff must be extremely sensitive regarding "sharing their faith."** These girls desperately need to experience the healing love of Christ. Even so, sharing spiritual truth with them must be done with great sensitivity and care, respecting their right to have their own beliefs and to determine if and when they will consider other spiritual beliefs. The story of the woman at the well in John 4 is instructive. Jesus models love and respect as he interacts with an immoral Samaritan woman, thus drawing her to God. He first addressed her felt needs, before introducing the spiritual solution.

6. **Offer psycho-education on the nature and types of abuse, the strategies of pimps, and the physical and psychological impacting of trauma.** These girls have been brainwashed and exploited in sophisticated ways. When they are helped to understand what has happened to them, the effects of this trauma on their body and brain, and how to heal, they will get better. For instance, most prostituted minors will experience classic trauma symptoms such as nightmares and panic attacks. They generally will have no framework to understand these experiences (other than to assume that they are crazy). They have no context to deal with their past trauma in a constructive way (other than denying or minimizing). A little education on these issues will go a long way. Learning identifying terms, such as *triggering, intrusion,* and *hyperarousal,* will help your survivor understand how and why she feels

the things she feels. She can then learn practical self-care strategies to deal with trauma reactions when they occur.

7. **Because prostituted girls have had to deaden themselves, including their desires and feelings, to survive "The Life," a huge part of their recovery is learning to identify and express their feelings appropriately.**

INTERACTIVE EXERCISE FOR THE GIRLS: SURVIVAL

After reading aloud chapter eight of *Princess Lost*, encourage your survivor to draw, paint, or collage the ways in which she has survived the streets. Provide a large sketch pad, journal, magazines, newsprint, scissors, glue, and glitter. She may want you to help her create her collage.

Suggest using as much detail as possible, and then, when she is finished, sharing with you (or her group) as she feels ready. Help her to understand that not only has she experienced significant losses, but she has also honed strengths that have been highly developed as a result of surviving the streets. These need to be included as well.

CHAPTER 9

∾

Love's Magic Potion

Hate may dress well and masquerade as love,
but real love requires sacrifice.

Princess Lost, *Chapter 9*

> Darkness cannot drive out darkness;
> only light can do that.
> Hate cannot drive out hate;
> only love can do that.
>
> —MARTIN LUTHER KING, JR.

A grandmother is chosen for the Christ figure in *Princess Lost* because the research tells us that for many survivors a grandmother was the safest person in their family of origin. She, more than any other immediate or extended family member, embodies safety, nurture, and comfort. The grandmother, in *Princess Lost*, represents Christ and his unconditional love for the princess.

The contrast between chapters eight and nine of *Princess Lost* is stark. Chapter eight concludes with pain and despair, as the princess cries herself to sleep, swallowed in anguish. Chapter nine shatters the gloom as Regina's Fairy Grandmother sings a magical and divine love song based on John 3:16, Romans 8:1–39, and 1 John 4:7–14. This love song inaugurates the sacrificial act of love that she is about to offer for the lost princess and the children of the caves. She sings:

> *The gift of love*
> *Fills a baron's purse.*
> *The gift of love*
> *Breaks up every curse.*
> *The gift of love*
> *Casts out every fear.*
> *The gift of love*
> *Stops the saddest tear.*
> *The gift of love*
> *Sets the captive free.*

The gift of love
Frees the blind to see.

THE LOVE OF GOD

The heart of chapter nine is the depth of God's love for sin-cursed humans. It is that powerful love of God that broke Satan's curse and set captives free. In a world stained by oppression, sin, and misery, this miraculous love song may seem like a fictional fairy tale. Sexually exploited adolescents in particular may respond with disbelief to the Gospel's message of love. Up to this point, they have not felt loved by God, but betrayed and abandoned by him.

Thankfully, the blazing flame of divine love cannot be extinguished by human pain or cynicism. In spite of human unbelief and demonic hostility, God will win the battle to redeem fallen humans back to himself. In chapter nine of *Princess Lost*, we find Fairy Grandmother proclaiming:

> "It is love that brings a thousand children into life. It is hate that seeks their death. I will bring the King's songs against your hate and stop all human tears!" she shouted at the monstrous goblin before her. With a fixed and fierce stare, she dismissed the beastly creature and, turning on her heels, angrily took her leave. The air in the cave crackled with her fury; the heavens rumbled with the force of her love.

> "I will win. Love will win. Death will bring forth life," Grandmother solemnly vowed.

> Then, with the softening of her face and
> the dampness of tears upon her cheeks, you
> could hear the faintest of melodies escape
> her lips. The graceful notes, lifted lightly by
> a gentle breeze, flowed out of the oppressive,
> dark cave and into the light of a new day.

Scripture describes God's love as so powerful, so victorious, and so undeserved that it is hard for us to fathom, let alone accept. For instance, Saul had devoted his entire life to destroying the Christian faith by persecuting and killing Christians. He was the worst of sinners (1 Tim 1:15). But, when he personally encountered Christ, he was so transformed by God's love that he changed the direction of his devotion to proclaiming the person and message he had sought to eradicate (Gal 1:13–23). After God changed Saul's name to Paul, the same Saul gave a most helpful explanation of God's love for hopeless sinners:

> *As for you, you were dead in your transgressions*
> *and sins, in which you used to live when you*
> *followed the ways of this world and of the ruler*
> *of the kingdom of the air, the spirit who is now*
> *at work in those who are disobedient. All of us*
> *also lived among them at one time, gratifying*
> *the cravings of our sinful nature and following*
> *its desires and thoughts. Like the rest, we were by*
> *nature objects of wrath. But because of his great*
> *love for us, God, who is rich in mercy, made*
> *us alive with Christ even when we were dead*
> *in transgressions—it is by grace you have been*
> *saved. And God raised us up with Christ and*

*seated us with him in the heavenly realms in
Christ Jesus, in order that in the coming ages he
might show the incomparable riches of his grace,
expressed in his kindness to us in Christ Jesus.*
EPHESIANS 2:1–7

This is a helpful passage for all of us who care for prostituted and exploited youth. As we have already discussed, the survivors we love are heavily damaged—physically, emotionally, and spiritually. As a result, they develop various maladaptive responses and defenses. They are often hardened, and appear hopeless. Humanly speaking, they are without hope! However, in reality, all of us are in a hopeless condition, apart from Christ. Ephesians 2:1–7 says that we were "dead" in our sins, following the destructive ways of the world. Ultimately, we followed the ways of Satan, the god of this world. We were enslaved by destructive urges. As a result we were, by nature, children of wrath. Our moral condition and sinful choices deserved divine punishment.

We are all hopeless and helpless in ourselves. But God who is rich in mercy, because of his great love for us, showed the *incomparable riches* of his grace by making us alive in Christ. The obvious irony is that, to make us alive, Christ had to die. What an amazing love exchange God provided for us!

The love of God is incredible and so different from human love that the English word *love* doesn't begin to explain this profound reality. God's love utterly transcends human love. In ancient Greek, there were four different words for love. *Eros*, the word from which we get the English word *erotic*, refers to sexual love. While *erotic* often has pornographic connotations in our culture, its Greek usage could, and often did, denote beautiful romantic love. At its best, human eros is based on discovering beauty and goodness in another.

God's love, most often conveyed in the New Testament with the Greek word *agape*, is dramatically different. Theologian Donald Bloesch articulates the magnificent nature of God's love:

> In agape, God loves us despite what we are and have become. We must not say that God loves us because of who we are, that He sees something in us that is fantastic and admirable. Sinners are loved not because they are beautiful; they are beautiful because they are loved. God loves not in order to enhance or adorn himself but simply because he wills to give of himself unreservedly to those who are inferior to himself.[118]

Bloesch's explanation of agape love helps us understand its transforming power. Sinners are not loved because they are beautiful; they are beautiful because they are loved. In other words, eros discovers value, agape creates value. God's love is, thus, not based on our worthiness, but on God's delight in giving of himself to those who have not earned his favor, but who need it. This is what makes it grace—unmerited favor. This is also what makes God's love for fallen sinners so amazing. Thus, Randy Alcorn admonishes us, "Never believe anything about yourself or God that makes His grace to you seem anything less than astonishing. Because that's exactly what it is."[119]

The love of God is so important that we need to explore it a bit more. In *Princess Lost*, Fairy Grandmother's sacrificial love was prompted by her sorrow over Regina's misery and that of the other children. "Because of her great love, her heart could not bear the weight of the pain of these children." She "would not, and could not, tolerate this demonic misery." Her heart broke, and her eyes wept over the children's suffering.

THE MERCY OF GOD

We Christians sometimes put such emphasis on the holiness of God and on God's hatred of sin that we lose sight of his mercy. In ministry to prostituted girls, it is essential that we view God's holiness through the lens of his mercy. These girls are most often filled with shame. They believe they deserve the intense pain they are experiencing. If they do not perform satisfactorily for pimps and johns, they are severely punished. Further complicating matters, most have done harmful, wrong things that should and do cause them to feel true shame and remorse. As a result, prostituted and exploited youth often become emotionally numb and hardened to their suffering. Drug and alcohol use further numbs them to their pain. They are detached, not only from their own emotions, but also from other people's benevolence. Their shame and their lifestyle isolate them from anyone not in "The Life," making them feel alone and unworthy of being truly loved and cared for.

These destructive dynamics are no mere accident. In *Princess Lost*, we see the goblins delight in human misery. We hear their evil malevolence as one hisses "the only mirth that I know is the cacophony of agony that grows from little dirty wretches such as these." This picture accords well with Scripture, where Satan is given the name Apollyon, which in Greek means *destroyer* (Rev 9:11). C. S. Lewis insightfully suggests that demons act based on two primary motivations: "fear of punishment and an intense desire to consume."[120] He explained the latter in terms of "a kind of hunger" in which demons spiritually "eat one another."[121] He supports this by noting that we see a similar dynamic among wicked predators who are driven to so dominate others that they virtually digest them. Prostitution and other forms of sexual exploitation surely represent ultimate forms of physical, emotional, and spiritual destruction in which individuals are consumed to feed evil's lust for sex and money.

It is precisely here, at the intersection of human and demonic destruction, that the mercy of God is most beautiful and powerful. *Mercy* refers to God's goodness shown to those in distress, regardless of the cause of their suffering. It is compassion in action, relieving another's suffering. Some of our suffering is self-induced through our own sinful choices, and some is created by the sin and oppression of others. Either way, God is shockingly merciful and compassionate when we suffer. He is specifically merciful when we suffer due to exploitation, oppression, and slavery. This is exactly the type of suffering that prompted God's mercy toward the children of Israel. They suffered due to the exploitation of Egyptian slavery: "The LORD said, 'I have indeed seen the misery of my people in Egypt. I have heard them crying out because of their slave drivers, and I am concerned about their suffering. So I have come down to rescue them' " (Exod 3:7-8).

God equally demonstrated mercy toward the children of Israel when they suffered from their own sin. Throughout the book of Hosea, God implores Israel to stop prostituting herself with other "lovers," which resulted in much suffering. He begs her to return to him so he can heal her (Hosea 6:1–3, 7:1–13, 12:1–6, 14:1–4). Even in the midst of Israel's stubborn rebellion, God was exceedingly merciful. He was moved to act on her behalf. Her pain, even though self-induced, grieved and pained him, because he loved her. "So My people are bent on turning from Me. ... How can I give you up, O Ephraim? How can I surrender you, O Israel? ... My heart is turned over within Me, all My compassions are kindled" (Hosea 11:7–8, NAS).

Similarly, in the New Testament, we repeatedly see Christ being "moved with compassion" due to human misery.[122] The Greek word used to refer to Christ's compassion (*splagch-nizomai*) literally means to have your intestines churning. The Greeks understood that, when a merciful person sees a fellow human suffering, one's compassion will cause an instinctual "sick in the stomach" response. When Jesus, the perfect, holy Son of God, looked at suffering humans, he responded with compassion: "When he saw the crowds, he had compassion on them, because they were harassed and helpless, like sheep without a shepherd" (Matt 9:36). Thus, biblical teaching makes it undeniably clear that God looks at prostituted girls today with great compassion and sorrow.

THE EMOTIONAL COST OF MERCY

When our hearts mirror the heart of God, we mourn with those who mourn (Rom 12:15); we grieve and weep over the pain and suffering of others (John 11:33–35). It hurts us when others are hurting. With the Holy Spirit's help, we feel what God feels for others. Being merciful is costly. Being merciful to the exploited and abused is especially demanding.

Phyllis Kilbourn articulates this well:

> A high emotional cost comes with caring for
> sexually exploited children. Listening to the
> children's stories of fear, pain, exploitation, suf-
> fering, and hopelessness causes endless mixed
> and energy-sapping feelings: anger, fear, help-
> lessness, powerlessness, vulnerability, sadness,
> pain, and frustration. Caregivers also grieve
> over the needless and senseless abuse of chil-
> dren who are so vulnerable—abuse that robs
> them of their childhood and innocence.[123]

Kilbourn goes on to make several practical suggestions for
caregivers to cope with the emotional cost of ministering to
victims of sexual exploitation. They include:

- Take breaks from the ministry so one can have adequate
  time for renewal, reflection, and restoration of hope.

- Recognize your own limitations in expertise and
  resources.

- Utilize support groups.

- Develop healthy peer relationships.

- Maintain personal and ministry balance.

- Maintain physical and emotional health through
  self-care.[124]

Listed below are three additional principles for coping with the emotional cost of offering mercy. We illustrate each of these through our daughter Abby's ministry to sexually exploited children in Uganda.

Implications for Mentors

1. Through prayer, place the responsibility for healing on God's shoulders. We have noted that, in Matthew 9:36, Jesus looked at the multitudes, saw their true condition, and was moved with compassion over their suffering. When we see the true plight of exploited children and youth, it is overwhelming. The needs are great and the resources scarce. Thus, the two verses that immediately follow Matthew 9:36 are important for mentors. Jesus says, "The harvest is plentiful but the workers are few. Ask the Lord of the harvest, therefore, to send out workers into his harvest field."

Throughout his earthly ministry, Jesus spent much time in prayer. Often, after ministering nonstop to needy crowds, Jesus went away to pray (Matt 14:23). Often praying all night (Luke 6:12). Notice the perfect balance Jesus shows us here. His heart breaks over the condition of multitudes, but he doesn't lose perspective. He doesn't allow the needs to overwhelm him. Rather, he instructs his disciples that, when they see the broken, they should pray to the Father so that he will send workers. In other words, we are God's instruments. God does the healing. God sends the resources. Healing is ultimately God's responsibility—not ours. Prayer places the responsibility where it belongs.

After nine months ministering to street children and genocide survivors in Uganda and Rwanda, our daughter Abby summarized the pain and brokenness she experienced.[125] Notice that her solution is not to quit caring and quit feeling the pain. Rather, she learned to carry others' pain in a healthy way, by not carrying all of the weight and responsibility. She did this through prayer to the God who cares, provides, and heals.

> The orphans. The street kids who must steal and rummage through trash to get by. The widows. The lonely. The eight-year-old girl who has been sold into the sex slave trade. The mother, who has lost her child and is now dying herself of AIDS. The underdog who just can't seem to get on top. The child who is forgotten at home. The community that is slowly starving to death because of drought. The child soldier who must kill and be beaten to survive. The woman who is divorced because she was raped. The marginalized. The abused. The suffering. Carry them in your heart. Carry them even though it is hard, and sometimes it will hurt, will really hurt. Carry them because sometimes they cannot carry themselves. Pray. Pray without ceasing.

2. Increasingly draw a sense of worth and love from God. Abuse survivors are fragile. They often don't understand or appreciate attempts to help them. Sometimes, they blame us instead of blaming their perpetrators. Sometimes they get angry or frustrated, believing that we should be doing more to help them. Abuse ministry is not the best way to feel like a hero or to garner love and self-esteem! Our worth and sense of being loved must come from God, not others.

In the Upper Room discourse recorded in John, Jesus prayed fervently for his disciples. His prayer reveals his sense of confidence in being loved by the Father:

> *Father, I want those you have given me to be*
> *with me where I am, and to see my glory,*
> *the glory you have given me because you loved*
> *me before the creation of the world. Righteous*
> *Father, though the world does not know you,*
> *I know you, and they know that you have sent*
> *me. I have made you known to them,*
> *and will continue to make you known in order*
> *that the love you have for me may be in them*
> *and that I myself may be in them.*
> JOHN 17:24–26

Strikingly, in the next paragraph, Jesus went over to the Kidron Valley and was betrayed by Judas. Then, Jesus's disciples abandoned him. Jesus's sense of worth was secure, however, because he was anchored in the Father's love—and Jesus's disciples learned from this. Later on, when the band of fearful disciples became bold apostles, they faced great persecution. John, the writer of the Gospel of John, expressed great tenderness toward the broken. He spent the end of his life banished to an island for his faith in Christ. It is significant that John refers to himself in the Gospel he wrote as "the one whom Jesus loved."[126] John's confidence in being loved by God was clearly a precious truth that sustained him through fierce ministry trials.

When Abby began building relationships with exploited street children, she experienced one particularly difficult week. A local politician and headmistress confronted Abby and called the police to arrest her and the desperate street children she loved. Later that day, as Abby walked with a young street boy named Patrick, she felt his pain as people cursed and insulted him. One woman shoved Patrick and Abby into a wall. Abby felt the pain, not only of the community rejecting these marginalized children, but also the pain of them rejecting her and her ministry.

These experiences required her to find her worth and love in God alone, and not the community. In the midst of experiencing human rejection and suffering, she learned to receive her worth from God and savor the joy that came from knowing she was carrying out his call to those he loved. He delighted in her work. In the midst of great challenges and rejections from the community, Abby declared:

> I am SO happy here. It is a different happiness that I am feeling now. Not the giddy, excited, joyful one that I used to feel when I was here previously and with the boys at African Hearts. I feel fulfilled and exactly where God wants me. Although sometimes I feel heavy, serious, and sad, the incredible blessing of being able to serve street children is a joy that is ever simmering within me.

3. Allow inadequacy and inability to drive you to dependence on God. Our best efforts will fail. When they do, it costs us even more to show mercy to the broken and exploited. Sometimes, we won't be able to break through the defenses of exploited youth. Sometimes, our words of comfort and guidance will fall on deaf ears. Some of the boys or girls we have poured our lives into will go back to the streets. These disheartening experiences can quickly overwhelm us, causing us to feel like failures. These setbacks tempt us to believe we don't have what it takes to help the exploited.

It's true. We don't have the power to heal the exploited. The good news is that our inadequacies and inabilities can drive us to depend on God, the Great Physician who loves the broken and is committed to healing them.

Even Christ, during his earthly incarnation, was utterly dependent on the Father. In John 5 Jesus is confronted by hostile Pharisees who had just tried to kill him for claiming that God was his Father. Jesus's response to them shows us how to let our limitations drive us to God: "I tell you the truth, the Son can do nothing by himself; he can do only what he sees his Father doing, because whatever the Father does the Son also does. For the Father loves the Son and shows him all he does" (5:19). Several chapters later, Jesus tells his disciples, "I am the vine; you are the branches. If a man remains in me and I in him, he will bear much fruit; apart from me you can do nothing" (15:5).

So when we are feeling wholly inadequate to help exploited youth, we must look to and cling to Jesus, the Good Shepherd who gave his life for the lost sheep (John 10:7–18). This is a difficult lesson, but one that we must learn if we are going to minister to the sexually exploited.

While God gave Abby some early ministry successes, it didn't take long for her heart to break in the discovery that, no matter how much she loved certain exploited children and sought to help them, sometimes she just could not rescue them. This pain drove her to a much fiercer, deeper dependence upon God:

It is confusing. I always seem to fall in love with the street kids that no one else would take. The rough ones who grab your arm and pull you along instead of holding it, who can't stop themselves from fighting with the other kids and taking drugs, and are constantly moody. If you were to ask me why I love them so much, most often I can't give a clear answer. I just see this fighting spark in them that is different than anyone else I have ever seen. I am drawn to them because of their deep desire to be known and trusted even though they just can't stop battling with themselves. Abdul is one of the first street boys that I absolutely fell in love with. He had big sad eyes that would always linger on you, waiting to see if you noticed him, waiting to see if you were going to give him love or another beating. It took him a while to trust me, but once he did, he would always be happy to see me and would melt in my arms.[127]

Abby worked with Abdul for months and finally got him off the streets and into their residential home. However, it did not turn out as she had hoped. She wrote:

Although we had warned Abdul in advance that we were taking him, he was still as high as a kite [on drugs] by the time that we brought him home. The other boys noticed and said that he should go bathe, that cold water would wake him up a bit. It's been over a week now and the drugs have worn off, but he still hasn't "woken up." No matter how many times I tell him, he can't get my name right, he cannot stop himself from grabbing whatever he wants whenever he wants it, he cannot respond right away when you talk to him, he gorges on food like a wild animal, and constantly fights with the other kids. I know that he is smart, but he is still living in a fog from which he can't seem to escape. It is as if the streets slowly got to him until they broke him down to a point that he doesn't even know that he can now get up. I am very happy that we took him off of the streets. I think he can change; I know that he can; it just breaks my heart to come across a young boy in which years of drug use, trauma, and abuse have already taken such a great toll. It is times like this when I know that there is nothing more that I can give to Abdul, and it feels like what I can and am giving is not enough. Only the saving power of God is able to change a life that has been so battered down. I cling to God's promise of deliverance. Please pray for Abdul.

We wish we could report that now, several years after Abby recorded this entry about Abdul, that he has completely re- covered and healed. In fact, he has not. However, despite slow progress and many setbacks, Abby has seen God's miraculous hand at work in Abdul's life and in countless other lives. The fact is that ministry to the exploited is God's work. We do it for him, by his strength. We must learn to trust him for the results, for "only the saving power of God is able to change a life that has been so battered down." He does change lives and heal the broken!

MEDITATIONS FOR MENTORS

Read Hosea 1:1–2:23, 7:1–11, and 11:1–12. How did God feel about the destructive consequences of Israel's prostitution? How must it feel right now for God to watch prostituted girls he loves continue to suffer as they remain in that lifestyle? How can knowing that God is infinitely more grieved than we are help us minister to prostituted girls? Be specific. What has God already done to deliver your survivor?

Read Hosea chapters 1–3 and 11. List some of the emotional and spiritual costs that Hosea and God probably experienced in loving and ministering to Gomer/Israel. Based on Hosea 1 and 3, list some of the physical and financial costs Hosea probably experienced in loving and ministering to Gomer. Share some of the costs you have experienced or that you anticipate in ministry to prostituted girls. How has this impacted you? Which of the costs are most difficult for you to deal with?

Read Hosea 2:5–7, 9–23, and 11:8–11. How do these verses describe God's work to bring back and restore Israel in the midst of her chronic spiritual prostitution? What are the implications of God's work among the Israelites for your ministry to prostituted women? What negative emotions or attitudes are created when you forget this truth? Be specific.

What are the practical expressions of love most required of caregivers? How do caregivers express mercy (compassion) to girls who are numb and hardened and refuse to admit their pain? Practically speaking, how does agape love transform prostituted girls? How can caregivers facilitate this?

INTERACTIVE EXERCISE FOR THE GIRLS:
LOVE'S POTION

After reading chapter nine in *Princess Lost*, encourage your survivor to share her thoughts, feelings, or memories that were triggered by this chapter. Depending on her spiritual receptivity, ask her if she wants to know the Scriptures that tell of God's love for her. If so, read these together. She may want to copy some of them into her journal. Ask her if there were ways that love has been distorted in her life. Ask her if she can think of times when she was shown true love. Are there ways that she has been scared, confused, or hurt by God, as she has experienced him through other people?

Encourage your survivor to draw, paint, or collage a picture of a time when she felt loved. What does love look like to her? What does it sound like? How does it smell? How will she know when she sees it? Experiences it?

End your time together with David's comforting poetry in Psalms 121:5–8.

CHAPTER 10

❧

Love's Bargain

She wore a simple white linen garment that hung torn
and limp over her shoulders. She had the look of one despised and rejected,
a woman of sorrow who had known deep grief.
Had you been there, you would have turned your face away
from the painful image of that great, noble lady—
struck, wounded, and crushed by pain that was not hers to bear.
The goblins howled and danced around her,
hitting and spitting with the venom of the damned.
She was as silent as a lamb. Love laid down its life for another.
This is the way of love—its sacred, sacrificial power.

Princess Lost, *Chapter 10*

> Some Christians are uncomfortable with the idea that God has been in a dark, repulsive brothel, that he could possibly be a witness to all the evil acts that take place there. Our investigators are not only comfortable with the idea—it's the truth they count on.[128]
>
> —GARY HAUGEN, IJM

Sexual exploitation is one of the darkest, most repulsive activities imaginable. We don't want to think about what actually takes place to children in brothels, strip clubs, and cheap hotels in our own hometowns and around the world. We don't want to admit that right now, millions of fellow human beings live in squalor and degradation as slaves. Thankfully, God doesn't shut his eyes to evil and suffering. To better appreciate God's active compassion for those who suffer, let's remind ourselves of how much sexual exploitation twists and perverts God's good plans for children. One writer demonstrates this in the sarcastic essay, *When I Grow Up.*

> When I grow up, I want to be a prostitute. I want to be used by men however they wish. And I'll say, "Oh baby, yes, I love it, I love everything about you." And I'll hold back my vomit and keep on my smiles to convince them, so they'll stop slapping me. But because I love it, because I love the taste of everything about them, they'll say I'm a slut, a dirty little girl who needs to be punished. They'll burn cigarettes into my skin, jab me anyplace they like, bloody my nose, blacken my eyes, laugh at my tears, hold a gun to my head, cut me, tattoo me, as their eyes grow large and excited. I'll scream and cry and beg because I can't act anymore.

I don't want to be riding a pink bicycle with a basket in the front. … I don't want to decide for myself whether to wait for marriage to have sex and remain a virgin.

When I grow up, I don't want to attend college, consider joining a sorority, or have my own apartment. I don't want to try different career paths or figure out who I am. I don't wish for a wedding day in a church or on a beach with bridesmaids, a dad walking me down the aisle, little flower petals beneath my feet. Who cares about baby showers or decorating a nursery? I don't want to learn to cook or decide between being a stay-at-home mom or a working mother. I don't want any of those things. Because when I grow up, I want to be a prostitute.[129]

SETTING CAPTIVES FREE

No child dreams of being a prostitute when he or she grows up. Sexual exploitation steals beautiful realities and strips freedom. It results in bondage and oppression. This leads us directly to the key theme of chapter ten in *Princess Lost*—the great price God paid to free humans held captive by sin and demonic oppression. Chapter ten recounts the gruesome murder of Fairy Grandmother by the goblins. This makes the opening of the chapter, a hope-filled song by Whistler, all the more ironic. Whistler sings:

> *She has come! She has come!*
> *To release captives,*
> *To recover sight,*
> *To set the children free!*

She has come! She has come!
To send forth as delivered,
The cursed children of the caves.
To proclaim the victory of Papa King!

She has come! She has come!

Whistler's song is based on Luke 4:18, "The Spirit of the Lord is on me, because he has anointed me to preach good news [the Gospel] to the poor. He has sent me to proclaim freedom for the prisoners and recovery of sight for the blind, to release the oppressed."

It is important to note that this is Jesus's first public message recorded in Luke. It summarizes his divine mission.[130] All four of these activities—preaching good news to the poor, freeing prisoners, giving sight to the blind, and releasing the oppressed—deal with giving healing and liberation to those who are in bondage, to those who have insurmountable, crushing needs. In Luke's writings, "releasing the oppressed" emphasizes freedom from bondage to sin and satanic oppression.[131] Thus, the message and work of Jesus is poignantly relevant to the sexually exploited. *Modern ministry to the exploited is a pure application of Jesus's divine mission.*

ABUSE, EXPLOITATION, AND THE KINGDOM OF GOD

To better understand Jesus's divine mission, we must understand it in terms of the kingdom of God. In Luke 4:43 Jesus makes it clear that the kingdom was central to his ministry.

"I must preach the good news of the kingdom of God to the other towns also, because that is why I was sent."

Scripture, from Genesis to Revelation, teaches that God is the sovereign Creator and King of the universe. God's kingdom refers to the place or sphere over which he rules. Of course, as the creator of the universe, God rules over all (Ps 103:19).

Yet, God's rule has not gone unchallenged. He created this world beautiful and perfect (Gen 1–2), but, early in the biblical story, Adam and Eve listened to the voice of Satan and rebelled against God, plunging the world into sin and death (Gen 3). Thus, the perfect world that God created is twisted and corrupted by sin. We live on a planet that has been in rebellion for millennia. The injection of human and demonic rebellion into God's creation has brought suffering, exploitation, and death.

The storyline of Scripture is God's plan to redeem fallen humanity through Christ, the King who died for his people. When Gabriel came to Mary to inform her that she would give birth to the Son of God, he proclaimed that this child would sit on David's throne, would reign forever, and his kingdom would never end (Luke 1:32–33). Soon after Mary gave birth to Jesus, God prophetically told her that this royal child would bring salvation, but he would be opposed so fiercely that her heart would be pierced as if by a sword (Luke 2:30, 34–35).

Sinful humans, ultimately inspired by Satan, the ruler of this current world system, have always opposed the rule of God.[132] This has created such widespread oppression and resultant suffering that, humanly speaking, the writer of Ecclesiastes said it would be better to be dead, or better yet, to have never been born (Eccl 4:1–3), than to endure life in this sin-stained world.

This helps us understand why the Old Testament's prophetic passages proclaiming the future birth of Christ emphasize that he will bring justice and mercy for the oppressed, enslaved, and broken. Below are a few of the more salient messianic passages from Isaiah:

> *A shoot will come up from the stump of Jesse ...*
> *with righteousness he will judge the needy,*
> *with justice he will give decisions for the poor of*
> *the earth. He will strike the earth with the rod*
> *of his mouth; with the breath of his lips he will*
> *slay the wicked.*
> ISAIAH 11:1, 4

> *In love a throne will be established;*
> *in faithfulness a man will sit on it—one from*
> *the house of David—one who in judging seeks*
> *justice and speeds the cause of righteousness.*
> ISAIAH 16:5

> *He will not falter or be discouraged till he*
> *establishes justice on earth. ... I, the LORD,*
> *have called you in righteousness; I will take*
> *hold of your hand. I will keep you and will*
> *make you to be a covenant for the people and a*
> *light for the Gentiles, to open eyes that are blind,*
> *to free captives from prison and to release from*
> *the dungeon those who sit in darkness.*
> ISAIAH 42:6–7

The LORD has anointed me to preach good
news to the poor. He has sent me to bind up the
brokenhearted, to proclaim freedom for the captives
and release from darkness for the prisoners ...
and provide for those who grieve in Zion—
to bestow on them a crown of beauty instead of ashes,
the oil of gladness instead of mourning, and a
garment of praise instead of a spirit of despair.
ISAIAH 61:1–3

Prostitution and sexual exploitation involve multiple layers of injustice and oppression: physical and sexual abuse, exploitation of the poor, exploitation of the socially marginalized, and patriarchal mistreatment of women and children.[133] Pimps and sex traffickers prey on economically desperate youth and parents. Pimps, traffickers, and buyers maliciously mistreat and abuse women and children. Violence and threats of violence keep victims from leaving prostitution. Thus, the inauguration of the kingdom of God, in which King Jesus brings global justice and mercy, is particularly welcome news for the prostituted and exploited.

For some, however, news of Jesus's coming is repulsive. From the moment of Jesus's birth, Satan launched a firestorm of demonic and human opposition. King Herod's futile attempt to kill Jesus by slaughtering Jewish babies was just the first in a series of demonic attacks (Matt 2:16–18). Throughout his earthly ministry, Jesus experienced fierce opposition, particularly from the powerful religious and social authorities who loved using their power to oppress and exploit others.[134] Satanic opposition to the King and his kingdom was so acute that Jesus declared that his exorcism of demons was proof positive that "the kingdom of God has come upon you" (Matt 12:28).

Opposition to Jesus did not end with his death and resurrection. It continues to the present. Though Jesus has come and inaugurated the kingdom of God, the fullness of his reign, the complete triumph over Satan and the forces of evil, is still in the future (Rev 19:11–21). The writer of Hebrews thus says, "God left nothing that is not subject to him [Christ]. Yet at present we do not see everything subject to him" (Heb 2:8). So, from the time Jesus came to Earth until he returns in triumph someday, there is a kingdom conflict between the kingdom of God and the kingdom of Satan. But, because Jesus has inaugurated his kingdom, the sure victory over sin, evil, oppression, and death has begun. John Stott's description of the kingdom of God explains this well:

> [T]he kingdom of God is God's dynamic rule, breaking into human history through Jesus, confronting, combating, and overcoming evil, spreading the wholeness of personal and communal well-being, taking possession of his people in total blessing and total demand. … Entering God's kingdom is entering the new age, long promised in the Old Testament, which is also the beginning of God's new creation.[135]

Biblical teaching on the kingdom of God gives an essential framework for ministry to the exploited. It helps us understand why there is still so much oppression and abuse in our world and why ministry to the exploited is so challenging. Yet, it also gives us tremendous hope. Jesus has come and launched the kingdom of God, a kingdom that combats evil and oppression and brings healing and hope to the broken.

Someday, Jesus's rule will be complete, and all evil, oppression, and suffering will be extinguished for all eternity. Until then, we citizens of Christ's kingdom are to live out kingdom values so that the world can see the character of our King and experience the transforming power of his love. This is particularly evident when we pursue justice and mercy for the oppressed, abused, and exploited in Jesus's name.

ABUSE, EXPLOITATION, AND THE CROSS OF CHRIST

In *Princess Lost*, the goblins abuse, mock, and eventually murder Fairy Grandmother by throwing her off the cliff and into a dark abyss. This poignantly symbolizes the abuse, public humiliation, and murder Christ experienced. While the Gospels tell us that humans were responsible for Christ's murder (the religious authorities, the crowds, Pilate, and the Roman soldiers), Satan ultimately inspired Christ's execution. We see this early in the biblical record when, immediately after Adam and Eve sinned, God predicted kingdom conflict between Satan and Christ, the "seed of the woman" (Gen 3:15). More specifically, we are told that, while Satan would inflict a painful blow on the seed of the woman ("you will strike his heel"), Christ would strike a fatal blow upon Satan ("he will crush your head"). This helps us understand why Satan himself entered into Judas, prompting him to betray Christ to the authorities who would have him killed (Luke 22:3–6).

Thus, the cross of Christ is essential for those broken by abuse and exploitation, because the abuse Christ bore is what breaks the power of sin and Satan. The prophet Isaiah stated this in graphic detail: "He was despised and rejected by men, a man of sorrows, and familiar with suffering. But he was pierced for our transgressions, he was crushed for our iniquities; the punishment that brought us peace was upon him, and by his wounds we are healed" (Isa 53:3, 5).

Christ chose "to give his life as a ransom for many" (Matt 20:28). The New Testament concept of *ransom* denotes deliverance, particularly from slavery. It depicts humans sold into slavery to sin, being bought from the slave market at a great price—the price of the death of the Son of God.

Furthermore, the death of Christ on the cross broke the power of Satan and allows us to be rescued from the dominion of darkness and transferred into the kingdom of light (Col 1:13, 20). The writer of Hebrews describes this in terms of Christ taking on human nature so that he could die. "Since the children have flesh and blood, he [Christ] too shared in their humanity so that by his death he might destroy him who holds the power of death—that is, the devil" (Heb 2:14–15).

The complete and final defeat of Satan is yet to come when Christ returns with his heavenly army, but the defeat has begun. Christ's death on the cross marked the beginning of the end for Satan. Paul confidently asserts that, when Christ died on the cross, "He disarmed the principalities and powers [demonic spirits] and made a public example of them, triumphing over them in him" (Col 2:15 RSV). The Greek verb Paul uses here denotes a triumphal military procession, in which the defeated enemy is forced to march through the streets. Christ's death on the cross sealed Satan's doom so completely that Paul describes it as a military triumph that has already occurred.

Not only does the cross of Christ purchase freedom for the abused and exploited, the cross also experientially connects

Christ with their abuse. Christ can relate to the physical torture. He can relate to the taunting, the torment of shame, the isolation and aloneness. Just as Christ was marched through the streets, modern-day abuse survivors often feel as if they are paraded past crowds of people who don't care.

In chapter ten of *Princess Lost*, we read that "the inhabitants of the mountain villages thought very little of the abandoned and hidden youth below." This describes the life of a prostituted child in the United States as well as abroad. Not long ago, we invited a young woman into our home. She had been prostituted for several years, beginning when she was in her mid-teens. We were shocked as she told us that she was psychologically triggered driving into our urban community because she had to pass by several strip clubs and apartment complexes where she had been sexually exploited. We had no idea that these sex-trafficking prisons existed in our very neighborhood.

The wonderful truth is that, while society at large often does not see or understand the experiences of those who have been sexually exploited, Jesus Christ does. And because of the cross, he also understands. This makes him a sympathetic and merciful Savior. Survivors can run to him for help and compassion. The writer of Hebrews tells us, "This High Priest of ours understands our weaknesses, for he faced all of the same testing we do, yet he did not sin" (Heb 4:15 NLT). Christ understands what it feels like to be betrayed, beaten, cursed, threatened, spit on, sexually humiliated (he was crucified naked), and tortured. The sexually exploited are not alone. Christ understands their suffering and cares so much that he volunteered to suffer in order to deliver them from their suffering. The cross of Christ is truly one of the most important truths for survivors of exploitation.

MEDITATIONS FOR MENTORS

Biblically, the kingdom of God brings justice, mercy, and healing for the oppressed and broken.

List some of the ways you have seen injustice, oppression, and patriarchal mistreatment of women in your ministry to exploited youth. Read Hosea 6:6, Amos 5:23–24, Micah 6:8, and Jeremiah 22:16–17. All four of these passages are written in the context of tremendous oppression and physical and sexual abuse. How does the biblical priority of mercy and justice for the oppressed, abused, and broken shape and strengthen your ministry to prostituted and exploited youths?

Scripture emphasizes that God loves and redeems shame-filled people, including prostituted women. Read Hosea 2:19–23 and 14:1–4. How do these texts show God's redemptive love for Israel in the midst of her spiritual prostitution? How does this truth impact you? How does it help your ministry to prostituted youth? In what ways do you struggle to really believe this truth?

INTERACTIVE EXERCISE FOR MENTORS: GOD'S LOVE

Following are some basic truths about God's love. Read each passage and copy into your journal the verses that move you. You can return to these for meditation at times when you are discouraged or need anchors of truth.

- God is love: Romans 8:38–39, Ephesians 3:18, Lamentations 3:22–23. True nature of love: 1 Corinthians 13

- God pursues us in his love: Hosea 2, Jeremiah 31:3

- God is a Father: Romans 8:15–16, Psalm 27:10

- God has a plan for your survivor's life: Jeremiah 29:11–12, Isaiah 43:7, Romans 8:17

- God is a healer: Psalms 103:2–4, Zephaniah 3:17, John 10:10

- God values each of us: Luke 15:4–5, Psalm 139, John 3:16, 1 Peter 2:9–10

- God listens to us when we talk to him (pray): Jeremiah 33:3, Psalm 18:6

- God is a rescuer: Psalm 103:4, Luke 15:4–5, Psalms 18:18–19, Psalm 27:10

- God suffered every form of abuse also: Isaiah 53

- God is more powerful than the effects of evil in your survivor's life: Joel 2:25–28, Jeremiah 29:11–12

INTERACTIVE EXERCISE FOR THE GIRLS: LOVE IS SACRIFICE

After reading chapter ten in *Princess Lost,* encourage your survivor to share any thoughts, feelings, or memories that were triggered from this chapter. What did she like or not like about it? Is there any part of the chapter that she wants to know more about?

Have her identify a time when somebody sacrificed for her (expecting or taking nothing in return). How did it make her feel? What did it sound like? What did it look like? Encourage her to journal, draw, or collage a specific memory—connecting to as much detail as possible.

CHAPTER 11

freedom

"This is your Grandmother's pool, you know.
She has fashioned and filled it with her tears."
He talked with a swagger in his voice,
for he liked to be the bearer of good news.
"The story is written in the ancient scrolls.
It is a tale from long ago.
They say it is the greatest love story ever told."

Princess Lost, *Chapter 11*

> Every emancipation has in it the seeds of a new
> slavery and every truth easily becomes a lie.
> —I. F. STONE

In chapter eleven of *Princess Lost*, Regina leaves the cave and is freed from captivity; however, she is not completely free. Sadly, she still responds, thinks, and acts as she did when she was held hostage. After her emancipation, the goblins leave the princess crumpled on the ground. She cries, believing herself to be completely alone. She's still bound by the distorted beliefs about herself that were created by her enslavement: "Nothing good happens for me" and "I'm not like others." She struggles to accept the good and beautiful things she is beginning to experience, even though she witnesses them with her own eyes. When she sees the healing pool, she simply cannot believe it's real. She tells herself she must be dreaming, that it's an illusion. This highlights the challenge that mentors experience in working with sexually exploited children and youth. Long after their rescue and emancipation, their minds and bodies remain programmed for slavery.

EXIT FACTORS

It's helpful at this juncture to note what research on domestic (North American) prostitution reveals about the most common factors prompting individuals to leave "The Life." One of the greatest challenges and frustrations for law enforcement, social workers, and mentors who work with prostituted minors is that survivors are often highly resistant to leaving the lifestyle. Those who do leave are likely to return to the slavery they have come to know so well.

In a study of female prostitutes in nine countries, including the United States, Melissa Farley, one of the world's leading experts on sexual exploitation, found that more than 88 percent of the women wanted to leave prostitution.[136] When these women were asked what they needed to be able to leave, they listed the following: a home or safe place (78 percent), job training (73 percent), treatment for drug or alcohol abuse (67 percent), health care (58 percent), peer support (50 percent), self-defense training (49 percent), individual counseling (48 percent), legal assistance (43 percent), child care (34 percent), and physical protection from pimps (28 percent). Research with minors reveals that the unmet needs keeping girls in prostitution are often related to financial, physical, emotional, drug dependency, and self-identity factors (e.g., "I'm just a slut" or "No one wants me").[137]

Leaving prostitution permanently can be a complex and lengthy transition, involving identifiable phases: initial exiting, role distancing, and new role embracement/identity change. At least one of six traumatic factors typically motivates females to escape prostitution.

1. A "close call," in which the victim personally experiences life-threatening violence

2. The death or injury of a friend or relative in "The Life"

3. Declining physical health

4. Declining mental and emotional health, poor self-esteem in particular

5. Incarceration or other legal consequences (though it generally takes multiple arrests and incarcerations for legal consequences to be a decisive exit factor)

6. Increasing disgust with buyers

Based on these motivators, mentors must intentionally do the following:

- *Advocate and provide for your survivor's basic unmet needs, including provision of home, safe place, and resources for job training.*

- *Be patient and persevere. Don't give up on your survivor, no matter her setbacks.*

- *Consistently demonstrate grace, and celebrate the "little" victories.*

- *Maintain your faith in God's power to restore and redeem.*

- *Consistently love, no matter your survivor's failures or negative responses.*

- *Ask God for His empathy and compassion.*

- *Maintain your own emotional and spiritual connections so that you can feel like the prophet Jeremiah:*

My eyes flow with rivers of tears
Because of the destruction of the daughters
of my people.
My eyes will flow without ceasing,
Without respite, until the Lord from heaven
looks down and sees;
My eyes cause me grief at the fate of the
daughters of my city.
LAMENTATIONS 3:48–51

FREEDOM FROM SIN: FORGIVENESS, GRACE, AND SALVATION[138]

Make spiritual care a priority in ministering to the sexually broken. Christ's power to heal is the backbone of restoration. We cannot fully emancipate these survivors until they have emotionally healed and been spiritually restored. The only *true* redemption for their hearts and souls is experiential knowledge of a God who loves them individually, a God who has a plan for their healing and a purpose for their pain. God's love is the only tonic potent enough to heal the effects of toxic shame. His is the only love powerful enough to shape a new identity and life purpose.

However, *it is imperative to be sensitive, gentle, and cautious in providing spiritual care to this population.* In North America and in many highly Christianized countries such as Mexico, Uganda, Kenya, and Korea, a high percentage of children have been sexually abused by parents and buyers who were professing Christians.

As mentioned in chapter three of this guide, many prostituted girls have also been spiritually abused. They've had pimps or clients who refer to God, attend church, and possibly lead in churches. How then do we introduce prostituted girls to Christ? Dawn Jewell offers a most helpful summary of this process by recounting the story of Myrto, a woman called to minister in brothels. Myrto describes Jesus waking her in the night, like a father infuriated by the kidnap and torture of his children. Jesus's message to her was:

> I want you to go and find my daughters who are sitting in bondage. They are waiting day and night for someone to search them out, someone to go into their dark and dirty brothels and call their name, someone to open the door and let the light in. Tell them their Father loves them. Tell them that they have been deceived and they don't belong there—they should never believe that they belong there. Tell them that I sent you, hug them like I would hug them, kiss them like I would kiss them, clothe them, feed them, and caress their hair like I would. Look them in the eyes and see what I, their Father, see. See their bright futures, see their beautiful lives, see them in their true home where they belong. Do not call them prostitutes because I have a name for them. I created them in my image. They are mine.[139]

Notice the focus of Myrto's ministry call—to be Jesus to these girls, to be his voice, his hands, his feet. As mentors, our divine mandate is to love in Jesus's name, not to *convert*. It is the Holy Spirit who convicts, draws people's hearts to

God, and gives spiritual life (John 3:5, 16:8–11; Titus 3:5). If the overriding goal of our mentoring is conversion, the girls may rightly feel manipulated and used. They may sense that they must spiritually "perform" to get the help they need, just as they had to perform for pimps and buyers. Perhaps worst of all, they may question how much you, and therefore God, unconditionally love them. They may question whether you will continue to love them if they do not embrace Christ or if they struggle with spiritual doubts. **The love and care offered the survivor in Jesus's name will point the way to Christ.** God's enduring faithfulness and sweet presence are powerful enough to draw a survivor toward faith in Christ.

Implications for Mentors

Myrto's story informs us in the following ways, as we seek to offer the love of Jesus to exploited girls:

- Reach out to your survivor and pursue her. Go to her, in the dark places.

- Tell her you love her (as you consistently demonstrate that love).

- Tell her that God sent you to care for her because he loves her.

- Show her God's love by the way that you consistently love her.

- Learn to see her as her Heavenly Father does.

- See and speak to her original design—a beautiful woman made in God's image—no matter how she behaves.

- Imagine what God can and will do in her life.

- Tell her how you can see God healing her.

One of the greatest strengths of this population of girls is their emotional intelligence. In order to survive the streets they have developed keen observational skills and the ability to accurately read others. Chances are they are more accurately on to you than you are to yourself! This might feel disconcerting in the beginning, but is actually an exquisite gift. As you create a relational environment of trust and love, your survivor will speak honestly to you. Her feedback, though painful at times, will give you many opportunities to grow in your ability to love. Let me give you an example.

The first interaction I ever had with a prostituted girl was with a seventeen-year-old adolescent in a juvenile detention facility. She was waiting for me as I walked up the sidewalk. She was stunningly beautiful with honey-blond hair and wide, watchful blue eyes. She was anxious and poised like a cat, ready to strike at the first sign of danger. I was silently impressed by her ability to simultaneously meet me, while hypervigilantly keeping track of everyone who entered and exited the room.

"You've never been here before" was her initial greeting. She was correct. Her words pierced me like a knife. I was stabbed with conviction. Here I was, a Christian counselor of fifteen years, pastor's wife, seminary adjunct professor, and mother of two daughters and yet I had never been to this juvenile jail. My response was something I have felt and spoken dozens of times since. "I'm sorry. You're right and I have much to confess—the shame is mine and it has cost you much. I'm sorry." I couldn't hold back my tears of sorrow and regret that I had *not* been there before—decades before.

Thus began our first of many visits. We sat on a dirty bench, in a lonely prison yard, as she poured out her story, her heart, and her pain. We cried together. We laughed together. Four hours later, when we were both spent, the guard came for her; she got up to go back to her unit. Looking back over her shoulder, she announced, "I'm usually brutal on counselors."

Another healing survivor of abuse and exploitation put it this way:

> I can bury it ... deep
> Cover it up so no one knows it's there
> Trample over it
> Push it further down.
> Pretend it's not
> Until I can pretend to forget;
> Then forget to pretend.
> Learning to ignore the pain
> The pain that still hurts to ignore.
> The ground quakes with so much buried treasure.
> It makes it hard to walk a straight path;
> The trembling makes it easy to fall down
> And then forget why I fell.
>
> The stifled pain, like a scream
> Makes me act like I do today—
> Affects my every move,
> My every thought.
> Even during my best make believe.

Don't make me. I don't want to.
So I will ask (not wanting to):
Dear God, be the Key to that buried treasure
Full of hurt.
Dig it up.
Help me face it.
God says, "Be who I designed you to be.
Open your eyes. Open your heart.
And FEEL."

With the horror dug up and above the surface,
close to my heart,
I no longer look down at my feet when I walk.
I reach up and ask for help to carry the burden
You wanted it! You insisted! Now help me!
Once I finally do look up
I notice other souls walking this earth.
Each struggling to stand,
walking over shaky ground.

My eyes are open.
My heart is open.
It hurts to feel.
I was made to feel. To feel the hurt.
To feel other people's pain.
To acknowledge all the horrible buried
treasure.

I believe. Help my unbelief.

As a mentor, read the Gospel of John and observe firsthand what Jesus said and what he did in his treatment of women and the marginalized. For example, he broke all Jewish social conventions in conversing with a promiscuous Samaritan woman, treating her with the greatest respect and kindness. He demonstrated sensitivity to the needs of her heart and offered "living water" that could quench her spiritual and emotional thirst forever (John 4). He was characterized and slandered as a friend of tax collectors and prostitutes (Luke 7:34). His love and care for prostituted women was so impactful that it caused one woman to give him an expensive gift of costly oil, anointing his head and feet. His feet were wet from her tears, and she lovingly dried them with her hair in gratitude for his love for her. Jesus, in turn, faced harsh criticism for allowing this "sinful woman" to touch him. Furthermore, he lifted her up publicly as a spiritual hero (Luke 7:36–48). Jesus protected, supported, and refused to condemn a promiscuous woman (John 8:3–11). He was fiercely condemned for loving and socializing with sinners as he taught boldly on God's extravagant love for the lost (Luke 15:1–32).

Once your survivor is curious to know more about Christ and his forgiveness, you can teach and clarify several biblical truths. The most foundational truths are: the nature of sin, the difference between true guilt and toxic or false guilt (things she feels guilty for that are actually the responsibility of her abusers), the person of Christ, the work of Christ on the cross for our salvation, and the means of forgiveness (Romans 10:9–11).

Some of the biblical passages we have found most helpful for explaining God's gift of salvation in Christ include John 1:12, 3:16–18; Romans 5:6–8, 10:9–11; and 1 John 4:9–10, 15–18.

FREEDOM FROM PATTERNS OF SIN: SANCTIFICATION

When we come to Christ and by faith receive his offer of forgiveness, God forgives us completely. Not only does God give us a clean slate, but he also washes us completely clean in Christ's righteousness. When God looks upon us, he sees us as his beloved children, cleansed and made perfectly righteous in Christ.[140] Believers in Christ have been freed from sin, forgiven, and offered eternal salvation. However, in this life, salvation does not mean that we will never sin again or struggle with patterns of sin. The Christian life is one in which we grow in grace. As we are increasingly transformed into the likeness of Christ, we experience growing victory over sin.[141] God invites us into a completely "new life." Of course, believers will not be perfect in this life. We will continue to struggle with sin; however, we can and should find increasing freedom from the practices of sin (1 John 1:8–2:1). Complete deliverance from the power of sin is in the future, when we are glorified in heaven.[142]

As a mentor, give very practical guidance to prostituted girls who come to Christ. Assist them in the process of spiritual growth. Foundational to this process is your own example of a vibrant love relationship with Christ. Abuse survivors most need to see and experience the reality and power of God manifested in your life—an incarnational witness based on the life of Christ (John 1:14). This is demanding, yet powerful.

Once a girl is ready, we suggest addressing the following spiritual disciplines: prayer, soul care, overcoming temptation, embracing a new identity in Christ, learning to walk in the Spirit, and spiritual warfare.

FREEDOM FROM FEAR: FAITH

One of the greatest challenges faced by sexually exploited girls is intense fear. Sometimes their fear reflects the effects of post-traumatic stress and anxiety. Classic trauma symptoms include nightmares, panic attacks, intrusive thoughts, and hypervigilance (anxious anticipation of a threat). These symptoms are largely biological and neurological in nature, and can be greatly lessened through individual and group counseling, education in self-care, and medical intervention. Mentors who are well educated in the dynamics and effects of trauma and who are sensitive to the girls' trauma symptoms can assist in trauma education and self-care. This type of education and treatment will, in time, reduce the fear and anxiety they experience.

These girls also need spiritual assistance in dealing with fear. Again, mentors best lead by example. Sharing some of your own past fears and how you have dealt (and are dealing) with them is most helpful. As an example, Sarah, one of our Mending the Soul mentors, was supporting a young survivor in our city's core. During their first visit, Mary (not her real name) described feeling chronically anxious and triggered by her frequent nightmares. Sarah listened, validated, and shared out of her own healing the things that had worked for her. She went on to explain how she, too, had experienced nightmares in the beginning stages of her recovery, and had many creative ideas about things that might lessen Mary's anxiety.

Mary listened as Sarah shared her ideas. Together they went to a fabric store where Mary selected fabric for her bedroom. They created a "starry sky" effect on her ceiling and hung framed, calming, and safe images on her bedroom walls. Sarah also supported Mary in feeling and thinking through the boundaries she needed to put into place with her roommates. Sarah processed and integrated the embedded "truth" of Mary's nightmares with her and together they created empowering "endings" to these scary dreams. Sarah intuitively offered to Mary what she herself had found most helpful in her own recovery. After several months of mentoring, Mary's nightmares eventually diminished and have now completely stopped. Mary is now passing on much of the same help she has received to other survivors.

Scripture emphasizes the importance of spiritual leaders providing an example for others to follow.[143] It is essential, however, that this modeling be one of integrity, which includes honesty about one's own struggles and failures. Not only do survivors have the emotional intelligence to see through hypocrisy, but they also deeply respect authenticity.

A wise mentor respects and validates the intense fears and anxiety of the girl she is supporting. Satan delights in stirring up fear and anxiety in irrational ways. Prayerfully seek to understand what factors are generating a girl's fears so you can help her address them in concrete ways. You can start by praying specifically with and for your survivor about her fears. Allow her to process her fears with you. Gently probe and discuss those fears, sharing appropriate insight and Scriptures. Countless Scriptures can be helpful in addressing various types of fears. Some to consider (depending on the basis for fear) include:

- Passages on the various attributes of God: Job 38–41; Psalms 25:1–3, 10; 27:1–3; 57:4–11; 65:5–13; 89:1–18; Isaiah 40:9–33; 44:1–28; 46:10–11; 49:7; 54:1–5; Romans 11:33–36

- Promises of God to care for his children: Deuteronomy 31:6–8; Psalms 31:7–19; 34:4–22; 46:1–11; 91; 107:8–9; Jeremiah 29:11; Matthew 6:25–34; Romans 8:28–39; 1 Peter 5:7

- Assertions of God's power over Satan: 2 Kings 6:16–17; Ephesians 6:10–18; Colossians 1:16, 2:15; 2 Thessalonians 3:3; James 4:7; 1 John 3:8, 4:4; Revelation 12:11

- Examples and admonitions regarding faith in God during difficult circumstances: Exodus 14:13–31; Joshua 1:7–9; 1 Samuel 17; 2 Kings 6:8–23; 18–19; Psalms 37:7, 56:1–9, 116, 118:4–9; Daniel 3:1–30, 6:1–28; Acts 5:17–42; Hebrews 11

One final way we can help our survivors find freedom from fear is to share stories of God working in believers' lives during difficult circumstances. Gary Haugen, the founder of International Justice Mission, a global Christian human rights organization dedicated to liberating the enslaved and sexually exploited, speaks much about the great challenge of overcoming fear. He notes that most of us need to see someone else "charge the darkness first," and then, quite amazingly, the "chains of fear" begin to melt away.[144]

Here's one such story of an abuse survivor charging the darkness first. You and your survivor may find it encouraging and empowering.

In 2007 we led a team of professionals from Mending the Soul Ministries and traveled to the Democratic Republic of the Congo to conduct healing conferences on abuse. In the past decade, Congo has experienced a series of foreign invasions and civil wars that have led to the deaths of more than five million people. These years of conflict, coupled with entrenched patriarchy, have led to epidemic levels of violence against women. According to a recent United Nations report, Congo has earned the dubious distinction of being the rape epicenter of the world. As of 2011, more than 400,000 women and girls are raped every year in Congo. And this is likely an underestimation of the violence against women in this country. Many of these women were publicly gang-raped and mutilated. Tragically, raped women are blamed for bringing shame on their husbands and families. They are subsequently abandoned and thrown out of their homes and churches. Sadly, experts agree that sexual violence against Congolese women is continuing to increase.

In May 2007, while visiting a Christian mental health clinic in the north Kivu district, we witnessed the most painful yet inspiring Congo stories. The orgy of violence in this region has caused many women and men to go insane. In the midst of this satanic cloud, a brave Congolese woman named Mama Abia stepped up to face the devastating evil. She recruited a small mental health staff and started a humble NGO (non-governmental organization) to treat the broken, in the name of Jesus.

Abia's husband, a pastor, rejects the patriarchal, cultural norms that give women lower status in Congolese society. He encouraged and assisted Abia in the work. They received no Western funding yet treated the most severe mental illnesses with their own meager resources. Rebels threatened Abia and her husband, repeatedly raiding the clinic and stealing the few drugs they had for treating patients. Yet they braved the risks and continued to minister to victims of sexual violence.

During our visit, we entered room after tiny, dank room, packed with shattered men and women. We sat and listened as they shared their stories. We cried with them. We prayed with them. Our hearts broke over the evil these beautiful people had endured.

One young woman stood out from the rest. Her name was Naama, and her face haunted us for the following year. Naama had been held hostage, repeatedly raped and impregnated by a rebel soldier. Her family brought her to the clinic with her hands bound to keep her from harming herself and others. Whenever she saw a man she would scream, "All men are dogs!" She eventually quit speaking. We took home a picture of her catatonic face. During our visit, Celestia held Naama and prayed for her. As she did, Naama grasped Celestia's pewter cross necklace and moaned.

A year later we returned to conduct another series of trauma and healing seminars. Abia and her staff were again in attendance. We were teaching on PTSD (post-traumatic stress disorder) and presented the *Mending the Soul Healing Art Handbook* that we had prepared for the conference. We had illustrated the chapter on powerlessness and deadness with an artist's painting of the face of this same young woman from the previous year. After the conference we asked Abia's staff if they remembered the woman and if they knew where she was. In unison they cried, "She is Naama!" which means *grace* in Swahili. They told of her miraculous healing. Apparently, a few months after we visited the clinic, Naama began to heal and to speak again, regaining all of her senses. As the staff loved and cared for her, they began teaching her about the love of Christ. She responded, embracing Christ as her Savior. Abia's team continued to care for Naama's physical, spiritual, and psychological needs, eventually reuniting her with her family.

Abia surprised us after the conference by bringing Naama to meet us. We did not recognize her. The face that had embodied traumatic deadness now glowed with a youthful and bashful smile. She said that she did not remember our visit a year earlier, but when she had begun to regain her senses, the staff had told her about us. They assured her that we were praying for her in America. Naama beamed as she recounted how God had answered our prayers. Celestia "just happened" to be wearing the same cross necklace she had worn the previous year when she first met and prayed for Naama. Celestia placed the necklace around Naama's neck—a symbol of the power of the cross to heal and redeem. Naama continues to grow and heal, raising her daughter by herself, trusting that God will give her a husband who, as she says, "is worthy of loving me." Today, Naama courageously walks into the jungle villages, helping the Congolese survivors heal, to accept and love the babies who have been born as a result of rape, just as she had learned to love her own child. Naama is our hero as she charges the darkness, "running back to the caves" from which she has come, bringing Christ's light and hope into the gloom. Of course, Naama's own bold "charge" of the darkness followed the charge of another: Mama Abia. After our caregivers conference in Congo in 2007, before we saw the miracle God would do in Naama's life, Celestia wrote the following and dedicated it to the women of the Congo:

> You have been raped as women, as a country
> You have buried husbands, children
> You have lost more than can be measured in
> your struggle
> You have been assaulted, violated, and oppressed
> You have cried and the world has not heard
> We have not seen or felt your pain—
> We have been numb and self-absorbed
> and for that we ask your forgiveness

We believe you have survived for a reason
To tell your stories
To touch lives
To be healed

They cannot take your dignity or rob you of
your value or worth
You are strong
You are beautiful
You are the voice this world needs
Nothing is more powerful than your stories
So may you testify
And may the whole world hear
In speaking, you will heal
We want to give you voice—
it will set you free

FREEDOM FROM SATANIC BONDAGE AND INTIMIDATION

For freedom Christ has set us free;
Stand firm therefore,
And do not submit again to a yoke of slavery.
GALATIANS 5:1

All who engage in Christian ministry must be equipped to withstand satanic opposition to their work, equipped to reach out to the victims of demonic oppression and attack. In fact, the word *Satan*, a common title used in Scripture for the most powerful of fallen angels, means adversary (Zech 3:1, Matt 4:10, Rev 12:9). It highlights his opposition to God (Matt 4:10) and God's people (Luke 22:31). Satan, as the god of this world, has great but limited power. He seeks to devour believers (1 Pet 5:7), to hinder the spread of the Gospel (Matt 13:19), to hinder Christian ministry (1 Thess 2:18), and to promote the persecution of believers (Rev 2:10). The Apostle Paul reminds us that our battle is not "against flesh and blood, but against the rulers, against the authorities, against the powers of this dark world and against the spiritual forces of evil in the heavenly realms" (Eph 6:12).

Spiritual warfare is particularly common in ministry to the sexually exploited. Prostitution is connected with the realm of Satan, as is slavery and bondage, abuse, and destructive violence.[145] Prostitution and other forms of sexual exploitation most powerfully exemplify Satan's character as an evil destroyer and deceiver.[146] Beelzebub, one of the New Testament names for Satan (Matt 12:24–26), was originally the name of a Philistine god (2 Kings 1:3, 6). It means lord of the flies or lord of the filth, highlighting Satan's moral impurity and filthiness. He perverts all that is good, beautiful, and moral. Much of the perversion, destructive malevolence, and callous evil associated with sexual exploitation cannot fully be explained apart from demonic activity.

Spiritual Warfare and Demonic Oppression

The following principles are taken from a presentation by Gerry Breshears, professor of theology at Western Baptist Seminary. Dr. Breshears has extensive experience ministering to those who are under demonic oppression and attack, including those who have experienced horrific abuse.[147] This is given for your education as a mentor. Sexually exploited youth are already dealing with extreme levels of fear and many have been spiritually abused. Therefore, any premature direct conversation about Satan and demons will most likely increase and not diminish their anxiety and will not be received properly. Great sensitivity is required to know if and when this topic should be addressed. At the same time, we must as caregivers be well educated regarding biblical teaching and ministry principles surrounding spiritual warfare and the demonic realm.

- Jesus triumphed over Satan and all his demons, through his work of redemption, particularly by canceling the power of sin at the cross (Matt 12:28–29, Eph 1:19–23, Col 2:13–15). Satan is already condemned (John 12:31, 16:11; Rev. 20:7–10).

- The principle of authority is that we are in the kingdom of Christ. Jesus is Lord and head over all power and authority. Satan has absolutely no legitimate authority over the believer. We are *free* from Satan's claims upon us. All sins are forgiven. All condemnation is ended. All previous vows, promises, covenants, etc., are broken when a person comes into Christ's sphere of authority (Col 1:13–14, 2:9–15). We must never compromise this principle by saying that sin gives a demon legal right to invade a believer or attach itself to our soul. Believe in God; disbelieve Satan.

- Our primary weapons against demonic strategies are faithful application of the fundamentals of the faith (Eph 6:10–20, 1 Pet 5:6–9). Light expels darkness.

- The only spiritual information to be trusted is from God himself. This comes through the Bible. All other knowledge, information, and experience are considered guilty, until proven innocent, and suspect even then. Be particularly cautious about deeper meanings or uses of passages out of context. These are the same methods the dark world uses. Any information that comes from demons is presumed a lie for dark purposes.

- Basic patterns of ministry are found in the Bible. Patterns that differ substantially are always suspect.

- Avoid *every* form of contact with the demonic, including astrology, New Age paraphernalia, demonic movies and music, charms, séances, games, and Ouija (Lev 19:26, 31; 20:6; Deut 18:9–13; Acts 19:18–20).

- Most sin does not need any kind of demonic involvement. Demons often claim credit for sin or a tragedy, trying to profess more power than they possess. Allowing this to go unchallenged may lead to an unwarranted sense of helplessness on the part of a believer.

- We must be very careful not to give Satan and his demons too much attention or credit. This can lead to fearfulness or overestimation of their power, a fascination with evil, or even a kind of satanic worship. Do not seek to know anything more about the demonic than is necessary for practical ministry. The Bible says nothing specific about demons' origins, hierarchies, territorial jurisdiction, names, or specific functions. That suggests that we do not need to know these things for success in spiritual warfare.

It also suggests that we curb our natural curiosity about such things.

• Believers can always confess (talk about) their sin, accept Christ's blood-bought cleansing, renounce sin's place in their lives, and recommit themselves as instruments of righteousness (Rom 6:12–14, Col 3:1–17).

• Believers may be deceived, accused, or tempted by Satan and may yield to these attacks (though they do not have to). As children of God, regenerated and indwelt by the Spirit, we are responsible. We also have all the power needed to resist Satan's stratagems (Eph 6:10–18; James 4:7; 1 Pet 5:7–9; 1 John 4:1–4, 5:1–5, 18–19).

• When we respond in our own strength to spiritual attacks, without Scriptural reflection or prayer, we may give demons influence in our lives. Apparently, an evil spirit can empower, energize, encourage, and exploit the sinful desires inherent in us (Matt 16:22–23, Acts 5:3).

• Following is a typical pattern of prayer to deal with demonically empowered desires. The specific wording is unimportant. Power and authority come from God and his Truth (Scriptures), not from words alone.

> *Lord Jesus Christ, I acknowledge that this*
> *(name the specific area of sin) may be empowered*
> *by demons and evil spirits. If it is, I want*
> *nothing to do with it.*

Lord Jesus Christ, I confess that you triumphed over these demons and evil spirits by the power of your shed blood that purchased forgiveness for all my sins, and by your death, burial, and resurrection that provided my new life in Christ.

Lord Jesus Christ, I ask that you send any demons and evil spirits away from me. Demon, in the name and authority of Jesus, I command you get away from me, now.

Lord Jesus Christ, I thank you for hearing and answering my prayer. Please fill me anew with your Holy Spirit so that I will be empowered to live in obedience to you and freedom from sin and harassment.

• Jesus is our example. When he was attacked by a demon (Matt 4:1–10), he refused to argue theology (could the devil actually have given him the kingdoms of this world?) and did not ask for information or details about demonic activities. Instead, he quoted well-interpreted Scripture and commanded the demon to get away.

• If believers continue to allow demonic influence, they may become entangled in a behavior so deeply that they may need help from other believers to escape (Matt 18:15–20, 1 Cor 5:1–5, Gal 6:1–4, 2 Tim 2:24–26, Heb 12:1–13). They could be dominated by a demonic personality in a way akin to a wife being dominated by an abusive husband, or exhibiting personality change or loss of a sense of personal control. This is particularly true when there is direct personal involvement with the demonic, such as in cases of ritual abuse or deep occult involvement. However, such a person will never be abandoned by the Holy Spirit or left to merely human resources, as in the case of an unbeliever (Ps 27; 90; Isa 41:10–16).

- Getting rid of demons in such cases is done by direct command to the demon in the name of Jesus Christ. One approach centers on the pattern of Mark 9:25 and Acts 16:18: (1) Dear Father, it is by your authority that we proceed to deliver [name] by the power of the Lord Jesus Christ; (2) [to the demon] In the name of the Lord Jesus Christ and by his authority, I command you to leave [name]. You have no right to be here; (3) Father, I pray that you will empower this rebuke I have just issued in Jesus's name. Preface the prayer by commanding the demon in the name of Jesus not to hurt anyone and to be silent. Help the believer reaffirm basic theological truths. Do not involve yourself in arguments or dialogue with the demon at all. All prayer is done to God in normal tones of voice. Remember, Christ's power, not yours, is at work. You are only his instrument. Demons are sent away by Christ's authority, not by formulas, rituals, or the power of their names, etc. One grave danger of deliverance ministry is a subtle temptation toward pride and power.

It is the will of God for every Christian to walk in the freedom of their salvation, through the grace of our Lord Jesus Christ, in the fellowship of the Holy Spirit and in the love of the Father. Satan seeks to fool Christians into thinking that he has authority to boss us around. He does not! Stop giving the world, the flesh, and the devil any opportunity to defeat you. Follow Galatians 5:1 and live free from sin and Satan!

INTERACTIVE EXERCISE FOR MENTORS

A solitary soldier believed himself a regiment
And so he died, as he saw it,
A whole army felled with a single ball.
Fools are made secure by egotism
But the wise, knowing all their weaknesses,
Gather into troops
To walk through Dante's mind.[148]

—CALVIN MILLER

The teaching in this chapter is mostly for your benefit as a mentor. Traumatized youth are already dealing with extreme levels of fear, and therefore any direct conversation about the satanic will probably increase, and not diminish their anxiety. As mentors, we need to be sobered by Satan's schemes to destroy and discourage those who are involved in healing ministry to the sexually exploited. We encourage you to create and maintain a support team that includes a professional counselor (as needed), a mentor, and good friends who understand your work and the costliness of mercy ministry. You must not neglect your own soul and self-care. Just as the girls need to be helped to not move into "HALT!" so do we; be on guard for those times when you are too "hungry, angry, lonely, or tired."

We have found the following guidelines for **soulcare** to be most helpful:

- For every hour of face-to-face time spent with trafficked girls, I recommend two hours of soul care. Soul care is the provision of silence and solitude that allows time enough for our own emotional connection, meditation, expression, and renewal. (I am filled most with the Scriptures and recommend copying them into your journal for meditative purposes. I reserve the left side of every page for my heart's anchor to God's truth—His word, despite what I am feeling or experiencing at the time.)

- Nurturing our interior life—our primary challenge will be summoning the "emotional courage to move through the inner space that leads to knowing oneself. The more fearless I become in the exploration of my inner worlds, the greater my self-knowledge and my ability to help (others)."[149] *What we avoid in ourselves, we will avoid in others.*

- Creating and maintaining "inner psychological space" so that we have the capacity to be present and "hold" the pain of another.

- Filling our heart daily with the truths of God's word so that we are solidly anchored in his promises, his pathways, his metaphors, and his wisdom; taking time to record the passages that move and fill me in a journal for frequent reference as I have need.

- Creating and maintaining our own healthy peer relationships so that we do not attempt to mentor from a place of emotional or psychological need.

Following are some basic elements of **selfcare** that everyone, especially caregivers and survivors, needs in order to be consistently renewed. As a mentor, create and model a selfcare protocol for yourself and then support your survivor in doing the same.

- Exercise

- Dance

- Meditation

- Quiet walks

- Hiking

- Laughter—friends, movies, and entertainment

- Hobbies

- Reading—poetry, fiction, and biographies

- Music—listening and creating

- Enjoying nature

- Pets

INTERACTIVE EXERCISE FOR THE GIRLS: FREEDOM BOX

Read chapter eleven in *Princess Lost* and discuss. Provide two cigar boxes and a wide assortment of objects, paper, and art supplies for your survivor. Have her label and decorate one box "slavery" and the other box "freedom." Encourage her to create or find objects that are associated with each box or life, and store the objects in each box. She can choose to share these objects and the meaning associated with them when she is ready to do so. This is an activity that your survivor can come back to throughout her recovery.

CHAPTER 12

❦

Love's Sparkles

*"Oh, Papa, I cannot forget the children in the caverns.
They are your children, too, aren't they? They must be set free, like I was!
But what can I do? I am just a child!"*

*"No, princess! No! You are not just a child. You are my child.
I have set you free so that you will carry the same passion and the same love
and offer the same sacrifice that was given for you.
When you are ready, and you will know when, you are the one who will go
back into the canyons from whence you have come,
taking your new sparkles with you. The sparkles will give you light and
guide your way. When you see those tiny diamonds,
you will think of your grandmother and me. We are in your sparkles.
We are in you. We will be with you no matter how difficult the path."*

Princess Lost, *Chapter 12*

213

Precious jewel, you glow, you shine,
reflecting all the good things in the world.
Just look at yourself.

—MAYA ANGELOU

Chapter twelve of *Princess Lost* is dedicated to Sarah, our dream
girl, a quiet yet dynamic young woman who is the inspiration
for chapter twelve in *Princess Lost.* Her story of healing and
redemption is compelling and unforgettable. Today, she is
one of our most effective MTS mentors—faithfully walking
alongside young girls who have known the searing pain of
neglect, abuse, and sexual exploitation.

Celestia's work with Sarah deepened our faith in God's creative provision of truth. No matter how hideous and deceptive
Satan's lies about our worth and dignity may be, God's truth
overcomes them. We've seen it firsthand.

A SUSTAINABLE MODEL OF CARE: SURVIVORS AS MENTORS

Sarah's petite frame and delicate beauty hid the effects of
monstrous evil. She had endured beatings, rapes, and countless other abuses at the hands of men, including some who
claimed to represent God. Their words, actions, and neglect
had slowly deadened her heart. The spiritual abuse Sarah
had experienced also poisoned the well of God's written
word to her—psychologically triggering her every time she
attempted to read her Bible. This left her in a paralyzing
double bind. On the one hand, she battled horrific lies about
herself and her "badness" because of her abuse. However, on
the other hand, Sarah could not use Scripture as a reparative

correction to the personal and spiritual lies that had been forced upon her.

In the first few weeks of our work together, I prayed that God would reveal *his* truth to Sarah, in a way that was powerful enough to dissolve the toxic shame that had deadened her mind and spirit. God answered this prayer almost immediately. He did so by giving her dreams.[150]

In the beginning, Sarah's dreams came in the form of intrusive nightmares that gave concrete images and feelings to validate the subtle forms of emotional, sexual, and spiritual abuse she had experienced. I asked her to purchase a sketchbook and designate it as her Dream Journal. After waking from a vivid dream (or nightmare), she was to draw the dream in as much detail as she could remember. She was then to journal the dream, recalling as much of the sensory detail as possible—the sights, sounds, and smells of the dream. She was also to record the ways her dream made her feel—both during the dream itself, and afterward as she was remembering it.

Sarah brought her journal to counseling and we would discuss the dreams that God was giving her. In the beginning, her dreams were hideous and scary—nightmares mostly. Then, over time, they began to change into beautiful reparative images of God's love for her and his cherishing care of her. Sarah and I could fill a book with her dreams and the gift of healing she has experienced from them. Slowly, with time, she began to believe again in God's love for her.

For the sake of time and space, I will share just one of Sarah's many "sparkle" dreams. On a Monday, following one of our counseling sessions, I informed Sarah about God's new direction in my professional life: that I would be leaving my private counseling practice in order to create healing resources and training for caregivers of sexually exploited children. I was gently preparing Sarah for this transition; and, unbeknownst to me, so was her heavenly Father. Several weeks after this discussion, God gave Sarah the following dream. He knew she would need reassurance and direction. I believe God gave Sarah this dream to help her envision her future as a mentor, and to reinforce her need to stay focused on her own healing until she was ready to help others.

Here is Sarah's dream; recorded in her own words:

August 2009: It was dark, damp, and horribly uncomfortable. I was struggling to move forward in what was a life-sized garbage disposal. I was swimming through scraps of moldy fruit and rotting meat. Huge blades protruded in a star-shaped fashion in the center of the disposal. There were girls, barely alive who were scattered among the garbage, wedged between each blade. These girls could barely move, having gaping wounds from struggling to survive attacks from the protruding blades. I was sure the disposal would click on any minute. I was working tirelessly to help these girls climb out. I made make-shift ladders out of the discarded fruit peels. ... As soon as I thought the girls were out they would slip right back down again, each time deeper into the sticky, moldy muck. As I traveled deeper into the pit to bring these girls back I became weaker and weaker, the sticky fruit juice became like glue, keeping me down.

Finally, I was able to help three girls out of the disposal, only to find that I was too weak to get out myself. I could hear the blades start to turn underneath me as I was gripping the rim. I had only inches left to pull myself up over the rim, but I did not have an ounce of strength left in me. I looked back down and saw more lifeless girls embedded with scraps of waste, awaiting death. I was tempted to let go and fall back to await my own death by dangerous, whispering voices from beneath, coaxing me to let go. I was so drained, depleted of hope myself, even for the girls who were now out of the garbage disposal. What was to become of them? They were near death it seemed, just from their unattended wounds.

Looking down, I forgot why I wanted to live, it was hard to remember that I even had known hope. I felt myself slip and begin to fall. I was suddenly in this lucid dream state, half-awake. It was completely dark and I heard a woman's tender voice say, "I have something to show you."

Then almost magically, I saw the emerald confines of a forest. My eyes searched all through the deep woodlands until I saw myself walking on a singular path that stretched through rivers and over mountains. My mind was trying to make sense of what I was seeing; a myriad of colorful shimmers that seemed to flow like dazzling rivers through the trees.

 I traveled long and hard on this path to get to her voice. The path was showered with shimmering footprints, sparkly shadows of handprints on tree trunks and mossy sitting stones. I was tired and worn out. When I finally came to her home it was in the midst of the most beautiful woodlands. These woods were exotic and yet very familiar—they gave me the feeling of home, although I did not live there. The woods were filled with children. From a distance, I could see children walking in and out of her home. Some were playing purposefully and others whimsically. The children had little homes and communities spread throughout the woods. A few were learning how to fence, others were baking, others were gardening, and some were just running and jumping.

I ran into her home and with great urgency and frustration I was explaining how I had little time, and that I needed her to travel with me to this garbage disposal that I had just left. I kept pleading with her to help me rescue the remaining girls. She expressed her desire to go but said, "I know my time, and it is not now." I did not understand and was disheartened and discouraged. She just smiled and reassured me that her time was called specifically for these children and their growth. They were everywhere—in and out of rooms, the woods, on playgrounds, painting, climbing, gathering, gardening, jumping, and reading. They were from different races and cultures—representing different nations! They all seemed to have a purpose, all having a special gift or talent.

She invited me to walk with her again. We were moving into a deeper area of the woods where more children were—they were playing, falling, laughing, crying, learning, and sleeping. Everything seemed so purposeful here.

She led me to an ornately carved wooden door. As she opened it I realized it was a tree, amongst other GIANT trees. They were redwoods with twisted limbs and rough bark. Her tree was taller than the tallest redwood and immensely thick; the best part was the color, it was bewitching—a deep, velvety brown. The leaves were the brightest color of green possible. Looking up it was as if a canopy of emerald jewels was suspended high above me. I could feel the texture of the dirt path on my bare feet; the weather was perfect. There was a perfect dewiness to the air and a fresh breeze, not an ocean breeze but a calming, intoxicating breeze. There was an old, antique box she retrieved from inside the tree. It had dark brown ancient markings with worn carvings on it. She took out a giant leaf (like a banana leaf) and some creamy colored leaf strips, like giant string. She told me to thread the strips through the giant leaf.

I was frustrated; it was hard for me to thread. The cream leaf strips weren't pliable and needed gentleness or they would snap, but they also required firmness to properly thread through this big leaf. I would get frustrated and set it down, and think about leaving. But then I would pick it back up and thread more. I was going too fast and had lots of slack. I made mistakes and had to fix it. She just smiled.

I was becoming aggravated. I just wanted her help and I couldn't believe she wanted me to thread a giant leaf! I threw down the leaf and stomped off deeper into the woods. She found me in the woods, offered me her hand, and with a smile we walked back to the magical tree. I began to thread again, still frustrated but sticking to it. She made me tea and talked to me while I drank. I became sad again and urged her to leave the woodlands and help me. She became somber and told me how she wished she could go but said, "I know my time, and it is not now.

Now is for these children in the woodlands." We started walking again and she led me down a nearby path.

As we stopped walking, we were still in the confines of heavy trees and greenery. With an elegant sweep of her arm my vision was opened to an endless expanse of forest. She motioned to a stretch of woods that was beyond my vision. It was like a dream within a dream. I could then see all these communities of children—they were dressed in bright and flowing fairy dresses. Even the boys had on flowing silk. Some children's clothing was exuding more light than others, and whatever the children touched they left sparkly colors behind. Some left more sparkles than others but all had sparkles on their palms, feet, and chest. I now understood what the shimmering trail I saw in the beginning was—it had been created by the footprints of the woodland's children! She explained how the children needed to learn how to find their own heart's sparkles and that is why her time was to be focused on helping them and in keeping the woodlands. She would show me how to do the same.

Today, in 2011, Sarah is effectively mentoring young girls who have been rescued off the streets—out of the garbage disposal that almost destroyed them. Sarah is sparkly and vivacious, full of hope and life. She is intuitive and patient and wise, leaving her sparkles on each soul she touches. And they, in time, will do the same. The intergenerational cycle of abuse has been replaced with an intergenerational cycle of wholeness and love.

A STORY OF WHOLENESS:
FROM BONDAGE TO REDEMPTION

The remainder of this chapter demonstrates the trajectory from bondage to healing and, eventually, to redemption. This trajectory will first be illustrated through the heartbreaking story of Dagny, a survivor of noncommercial sexual exploitation that was not criminal, but was just as damaging. In some ways, sadly, her story is more the "typical" story of sexual exploitation. Most often, these stories are never told. Following Dagny's story, we demonstrate how mentors can understand, step into, and utilize this same bondage to redemption trajectory, for purposes of wholeness and healing.

Dagny's story is a gripping true account of honesty and courage, of healing and redemption. Today, Dagny directs our Phoenix-based operations for Mending the Soul Ministries. She is one of our most effective and potent facilitators, presenters, and mentors. She is passionate, joy-filled, hopeful, optimistic, loving, Christ-centered, and persevering in her work with survivors. Her story is spoken so that others might share in her courage—speaking their stories of pain in order to heal.

Dagny's story of early childhood abuse, emotional neglect, and the ensuing relational vulnerabilities created in a young girl, is told in categories of the typical strategies of pimps and predators who enslave girls in lives of sexual bondage. They recruit, break, and maintain. We have added two additional categories that give "the rest of the story": healing and redemption. Her story is important for us to know, because it widens the net of our care and concern to include *all* girls who grow up vulnerable to the seductive and manipulative exploitations of others because of early childhood abuse and neglect.

Here is her story; recorded in her own words:

Being used as an object for someone's sexual gratification is humiliating and degrading. No one would choose
that. I would never have chosen that. I did not know, as
a child, that I was to be loved and cherished. I had been
taught differently. I had been treated differently. Because
my body didn't fit the mold of what was actually worthy of
love in my family, I grew up believing that, because of the
way I looked, I was the exception and, therefore, unworthy of love. This was my most dangerous vulnerability. As a
young adult, I enthusiastically walked into a relationship
with hopes that it would diminish all that I was taught as
a young girl about my self-worth. I never considered that
my feelings of worthlessness were, in part, my greatest
vulnerability, and that I would be quickly manipulated
into an object to fulfill others' perverse sexual fantasies.

Recruit

I was twenty-one years old when I met him. We met at
my office. I was working as a receptionist; he was a well-
respected and successful businessman. He was well
known in his field and seemed to have it all together. I'll
admit, he was a bit old for me. Okay, he was almost the
same age as my dad. I didn't really pay much attention to
that fact. I didn't realize how naive I was and how easily I
could be manipulated. I had always been told I acted old
for my age. When he came in, he always flirted, and I was
secretly flattered, but never wanted to get my hopes up.
I would reason that he acted the same way with all the

receptionists in every business he visited. It was just his way of being nice, and I did think he was nice.

Over a few months, we became more and more comfortable with each other. There was this easy, good-natured banter that went back and forth between us. His meetings in my employer's office became more frequent. My heart always skipped a beat every time I saw him coming. I inwardly wished we could spend the afternoon just goofing off. I didn't want our conversations to end when he had to go into his meeting or leave for his next appointment. I really enjoyed the playful interaction we had together. *I had never had that sort of attention from a man before, and I really liked it.*

One day, he came in to the office, but he didn't have a meeting. It was the week before Thanksgiving. He said he had come in *just to ask me something*. He wanted to know if I had plans for Thanksgiving, and, if not, would I like to spend it with him? My roommate was out of town, my parents lived in another state, and actually I was dreading my first Thanksgiving away from home. With all those reasons, combined with the fact that I really liked him, it was easy to give him a resounding yes! He said he would pick me up Thanksgiving morning for breakfast. Perfect!

I was ready early and sat nervously as I waited for him to arrive. I wasn't quite sure what to expect. We had talked quite a bit when he came into the office, but I really didn't know a lot about this guy except that he was really nice and he seemed to actually like me. One of the girls in my office noticed that he frequently talked with me while he waited to go into his meetings. She told me she thought he was cute. She said if she wasn't married, she might go for him herself. She was a very attractive woman, so her comments made me feel even more special that he had asked me out. He showed up right on time, was nicely dressed, and very polite. We drove to a restaurant located uptown, which was about thirty minutes away from where I lived. During breakfast, it was a little awkward—different than it had been at the office. I'm not sure why, but it just was. Maybe it was because we were alone. After breakfast, he asked if I wanted to go over to his house, which was very close by. I didn't really know what to say. I knew my mom would tell me it was a bad idea, but I really didn't want to be alone, so I said, "Sure."

He turned on the television, but I don't really remember watching it. What I do remember is that, at some point, he asked me if I would give him a back rub. I really didn't feel comfortable with that and tried to get out of it by telling him I didn't know how. He assured me it was no big deal, and he just knew I would be really good at it. He offered to give me a back rub to return the favor. I declined, and was thankful he didn't push the issue. The thought of him rubbing my back scared me to death. I didn't want anyone touching me because they might feel the ugliness my clothes were covering up. I didn't want to spoil anything; I was having such a great time.

Since it was Thanksgiving, I remember asking him about his family. He said he had a son who was married and lived in town, and he would possibly go over there to see him later. He never did. We ended up spending the whole day together. Early in the evening, we went out to get some dinner at a restaurant around the corner. Out of the blue, during our casual conversation, he bluntly stated that men expect something from women when they take them out and spend money on them. I was suddenly very uncomfortable. What was I supposed to say to that? I knew what the "something" was that he was talking about. I didn't even want him to touch my back. How would I get out of this one? The day had been so much fun. I didn't want to ruin my chances of spending time with him again. I was so confused. I don't remember saying anything at all. Fortunately, that conversation didn't continue, and we moved on to other things.

After dinner, we got into his car so he could drive me home. We had been together the whole day, and now it was almost over. At this point, I was very comfortable being around him. I had pushed out of my mind his earlier comment and was just enjoying our last few minutes together. About halfway home, something started to feel strange. I couldn't put my finger on it, but I could feel it. He started talking out loud, but it was like he was talking to himself and not to me. I heard him mumble something about what he thought I would feel like. Before I knew what was going on, he reached over and grabbed me. We were alone in his car, not in a crowded restaurant. It was dark outside, and no one could see inside the car. I thought people were supposed to ask permission before doing something like that. I didn't know what to do. I wanted to hit him or scream out and tell him that what he was doing wasn't right, that I didn't like it. I remember being afraid that if I got mad I would ruin everything—we had had such a good time. If I stopped him, I feared he would never want to see me again. I just sat there frozen while he touched me. I didn't like that he felt he could just do that to me, but at the same time *I had a longing to be loved.*

About a week later, he asked me out again. For our second date, we went to the racetrack to watch NASCAR. I had never been before. It felt exhilarating being outside on a chilly day, with the sounds all around, combined with the fact that I was with a guy on a second date! He guided us to a seat high up in the stands; not too many people were around us. He had brought a blanket and asked me if I would like him to wrap it around me. I thought that was very sweet and said yes. It never occurred to me that he had his own reasons for bringing a blanket—that it was preplanned, the execution of his selfish desires. He stepped behind me and wrapped the blanket around, holding it closed with one of his hands. The other hand he kept inside on my shoulder. After a few minutes, he gently kissed me on the neck and whispered into my ear asking if he could touch me under the blanket. My initial response was to tell him he was crazy, to remind him we were in public. I was really uncomfortable with the whole idea. I wondered how was I going to be able to tell him "no." He had already touched me before, and, even though I didn't give him permission, I also didn't stop him. I was afraid—afraid of letting him touch me and afraid of ruining things if I didn't. I ended up softly and unconvincingly saying "okay," which was good enough for him. He kept his hands on me for what seemed like forever. Occasionally, he would whisper to me how wonderful I felt. My whole body was responding to him, but inside I felt dirty and confused. I wanted to feel wonderful, but I didn't. I can remember looking around at the people who were in our vicinity and wondering what they were thinking about me. I was sure they knew.

Things moved very quickly from that point on. After the race that day, he took me back to his house, where we had sex. I don't remember being asked; it was just expected. As I look back, I can see that there is no way I could have said no to him. I'm sure his mind was planning and preparing the whole time he was touching me under that blanket. Afterward, as we lay in his bed, I started to cry. He, in a very annoyed tone, asked me what was wrong. I made up some lame excuse so I wouldn't look totally stupid. I didn't even really know why I was crying at the time. As I think back on it now, I believe it was because I knew I had just been used. I wanted to be worth more than that, but I wasn't. One thing I did understand loud and clear at that moment: Crying was not going to be tolerated in this relationship if it was to continue.

We kept seeing each other, but after our second date, we stopped going out; we would just stay at his house. He said he liked staying in, and I didn't really mind. He no longer picked me up; I drove myself. He always sounded very sweet when he called to invite me over. He made it seem like he was making special time for me. I didn't stay the night anymore; he told me he couldn't sleep well with anyone else in his bed. Eventually, we stopped using his bedroom altogether. I remember telling myself one time that I would never want to marry him. I now realize that was the only way I could protect myself from the thought that he would never actually want to marry me. The reality was there were no more visits to my office where we would talk and laugh, because he didn't need to do that. There were no phone conversations except when he called to have me come over. There was very little he did for me, because he got what he needed without doing those things. I was not being pursued; I was being used, abused. Of course, I can see that now, but I didn't know this at the time. I still believed he cared for me. I still held on to the belief that I might be special to him. He often gave me compliments, but as I hear them replay in my head, they were about my "performance" and not about me. Today, I can see that he was sending a very deliberate and calculating message so he would be able to manipulate me into doing whatever he wanted while making me think he actually cared. It was covert; it was under my radar. It was so gradual that I never realized I was steadily moving further into his cloud of darkness.

Break

Pretty early on, he introduced pornography into the relationship. Drugs came in a bit later. The longer I was with him, the more and more intense and perverse his desires became. He demanded more of me that sickened me while, at the same time, making me feel as if I was the only one in the world who was there for him. This was my trap. I didn't want to disappoint him; I didn't want to be alone. Little by little, I grew numb to the things he wanted me to do as that cloud of darkness grew darker. Even on the rare occasion that I voiced some resistance, I always eventually did what he wanted. It seemed he always got his way no matter how I felt. At work and with my friends, I acted like such a strong person. None of them would have believed me if I told them what was going on. I never said anything to any of them about this relationship. When I look back on it now, it seems as if I was living a double life: one in the daytime and the other in the dark. My friends knew nothing about him.

I had met a few of his friends on different occasions. Most of them were married, and they would drop by to do a line of coke before heading out to the bar to pick up some young girl so they could "get laid." One particular night, a little later than normal, one of his married friends came by. This guy was a real player; he was always telling stories of picking up girls and what he would do to them in the car or in the parking lot. I didn't really think about why he was there; it didn't seem particularly odd or uncomfortable to me. At first we just sat around, talking and laughing.

As I think back on that night, I can remember the way we were all sitting in the living room; his friend was crowded next to me on the sectional sofa while my "boyfriend" was a few feet away on the other end. I never considered that it was all a setup until now, as I relive those memories back in that room. Oh, how I wish I could just confront him, yell, scream, and tell him how sick he really was. Who knows how long he had been planning this? It was a giant step deeper into the darkness, and I felt powerless. It was like I didn't really have control of my own thoughts or actions when it involved him. As I look back now, I can say that I hate that I fell for his manipulation! I hate that he was able to do the things to me that he did! I hate that he thought I was a consumable commodity for his use and disuse!

Maintain

That night was the night he first pimped me out to one of his friends. I just have to say that I really still hate using those words to describe what happened. I know they are accurate, but in my own toxic shame, I still don't want to use them. I want to soften the words so they don't hurt or embarrass me as much. He always used the words "take care of," and that seems so much more acceptable—even helpful, loving. However, softening the words will not speak truth and, no matter how he said it, the truth is that he prostituted me. I can remember him saying, "He and his wife haven't been getting along, and can't you please take care of him? You are the only one who can make him feel better." His friend was just looking at me, smiling and waiting. I knew I hadn't really been asked; it was an expectation. I'm sure I was incredibly scared, but I can't really remember. I wasn't feeling anything. It does make me sick now, though. I remember that all three of us stayed in the room. He sat there and watched as I "took care of" his friend. I remember the two of them talking about it afterward. I remember that I sat there and listened to them talk.

They were saying things they thought were supposed to be compliments, I presume. They don't seem anything like compliments from where I sit today, but, at the time, I can see how those sexualized comments were the tools used to manipulate me into deeper and deeper levels of perversion. It was to make me feel good about accomplishing something, as if I were in control. Today, I know that it was a sick and perverse way of achieving his abusive goal of total control over me for his exploitive pleasure. These perverted compliments were a part of our exchange; this was what I got from our relationship.

As the relationship and depth of perversion deepened, other men were brought in. There was always a reason given: This one's wife is out of town for the weekend; this one has been alone for a long time; this one just needs a release. The months and years that followed became a blur, but two events are very vivid in my memory. The first was when I was introduced to his son, who was a year or two older than me. I was sickened by the thought of performing sexual acts for his son and flat-out refused to even talk about it. For some reason, he didn't push it. I remember it made me feel strong that I said no. The second very significant memory was meeting Sandy. Out of all the friends I was prostituted to, his is the only name I remember. This time, we went alone into a different room, and he demanded to have intercourse. I didn't want to, but felt powerless to say no. I remember being very scared as I walked into the bedroom. I also remember hearing my "boyfriend's" voice from the other room telling me that I was "really going to enjoy this." He was very wrong. Sandy forcefully raped me; he forced himself inside me. It was very painful. That night, a part of me died. I can remember feeling like I was no longer in my body. I separated myself from everything that was happening to me. I stared at the ceiling waiting until he was done, enduring the pain and hating every moment I was in that room. I had met Sandy before, and he had always seemed like a really nice guy, the kind who would never use someone that way. His actions that night finished off my ability to trust any man again, even the "nice" ones.

Heal

The things done to me in this relationship were atrocious. I live with those memories. They intrude into my life in one way or another almost every day. There are a few scars I still carry physically because of my abuse. But, most of the damage done to me is hidden, below the surface, in my soul where it is difficult to see. It hurts to go back to those places, to recognize the manipulation and coercion, to itemize all that was done to me and stolen from me because of this abusive man. To relive those things without the cloud of darkness allows me clarity of vision, but also requires me to feel the pain, and it hurts terribly. It is my grief. I will continue to tell my story, to feel it, and to grieve it. To name the abuse that I have experienced, and to itemize my losses, feeling and expressing them, is an important part of my healing.

During the three years of that relationship, he used many forms of manipulation, including public humiliation, blackmail, and a suicide threat on top of the endless mind games, emotional abuse, and sexual exploitation. After we had been together almost two years, he married. He had been seeing this woman the whole time we had been together. It hurts that I was so blind; it hurts that I never considered her as I continued to see him; it hurts that I couldn't see the damage that was being done within me that would affect my own marriage; it hurts that I have to fight every day to trust a man who actually loves me well and respects me and my body; it hurts that, for years, I lived behind a mask and didn't even recognize that I was broken. Most of all, it hurts that there is evil in this world that would take the innocence of a young woman, disregard her original design, and consume her without thought of her true identity: the very daughter of the King!

God did make a way for me to get out of that abusive relationship, and I am forever grateful to him for sending my husband. There was still some light in my soul that longed for the love that I had been created for and only dreamed of as a child, but felt I was unworthy of receiving. My husband came into my life with eyes that saw me as worthwhile and lovable—someone to be cherished. He says that, the first time he saw me, he knew I was "the one." He says it was as if all time stopped and everyone else disappeared; only the two of us were in the room as we moved around in slow motion, not even speaking to each other. Through his gentle kindness, I was allowed to begin to experience what it was like to have a man offer his heart to me instead of taking everything possible from me. I experienced love that was not only spoken through words, but also carried out in his acts of adoration. This truth of how I was created to experience love gave me strength, and I can clearly remember the day I walked away from my abuser.

I have never looked back. When my "boyfriend" called the last time, I went with my own agenda, not to fulfill his. I was going over to his house to say goodbye. I wasn't quite sure how I was going to do it. I still felt this sense of control that he had over me. I walked up to the door with the same anxious feeling I had every time before. It had been weeks, possibly months, since I had last been there. As we started to talk, I distinctly remember the feeling that a cloud was being lifted. I remember thinking that I had never heard him talk this way before; he was making absolutely no sense! The things he was saying were so strange, and I didn't agree with him at all. He had always seemed so intellectual, and suddenly he sounded like a complete idiot. It was at that moment that I knew I had to go, and I told him I needed to leave. He tried to convince me to stay. His words only convinced me more that it was time for me to go. After arriving no more than fifteen minutes earlier, I found myself walking out the front door, never to set foot in that house again. I can remember the feeling of freedom as I walked away. I never even looked over my shoulder to see if he was standing there.

It wasn't until twenty-five years later that I realized, through education, that what I had experienced was abuse. I finally stepped onto the healing path of my journey with the Lord. I am grateful to God for never leaving me, even at those times when I didn't realize he was there. I didn't accept Jesus as my Lord and Savior until twenty years after I left my abuser. I can see now that it was a long, painful period without the recognition of Jesus being by my side, but, today, it has made me all the more aware as I now walk with, depend on, and cherish him every day of my life.

It is still painful today to see how my abuse has affected my marriage and distorted what God had designed for our intimacy. This journey of healing is very hard, extremely frustrating, and sometimes feels impossible. But God has promised that he will heal this brokenness! In my darkest of days, I cling to that promise he's made to me. On the brighter days, I allow my wonderful and loving husband to cherish me, even though I struggle to accept it. I am still often unable to understand where he sees beauty in this mess. It makes him sad when I share that with him. Someday, I know I will be able to fully accept his words and his touch without fear of being transported back to that place of pain. Every day, we are closer to the true marital intimacy that God has designed for us to experience together.

Redeem

Today, God has equipped me with an understanding of abuse and its effects, and of his promise of redemption. He equipped me by teaching me through my own story of his love for me, and is now using me, and my story, to help others. I think of the countless women and men I come in contact with who feel as I felt: worthless and unlovable. I know they are not, because I know I am not. I know they are fearfully and wonderfully made, because the Lord taught me that I am fearfully and wonderfully made. I recognize pain in the eyes of others because I remember the reflection of the hollowness that was in my own eyes.

Experiencing God's healing and knowing his promises allow me to share the hope he gave me, which he offers to everyone—even when I can't tell them directly. There are some people he has placed specifically in my heart; I carry their pain daily and continue to be changed by their pain. I pray and fast for them: those who can't yet accept that they are an amazing gift to this world. Through my healing, God has given me a voice that will not keep silent when faced with abuse. He has given me a spirit that encourages and empowers others in their own personal journeys. But, most of all, he has given a way for me to grow daily in my ability to love the Lord my God with all my heart, with all my soul, and with all my mind, and to love my neighbor as myself (Matt 22:37, 39). He continually teaches me, first of all, to love and trust him at levels I often cannot understand, and then to truly love myself so I am able to allow him to pour out the fullness he has given me into the lives of others. What a humbling experience it is each and every time I realize he has privileged me to share his greatness and amazing love with others.

Dagny's story gives tremendous hope to others who have been deeply wounded by sexual exploitation. By God's grace, they can be rescued and restored, making their way out of the dark caves. Not only can they survive, but, in time, thrive—emotionally, relationally, and spiritually, equipped to charge back into the caves for the rescue and redemption of others.

We particularly respect Dagny's invincible sense of mission. In spite of many years of degrading abuse and exploitation, which filled her heart and mind with shame, lies, and hopelessness, God has now given her "a voice that will not remain silent about abuse." She is using her voice to give hope to the hopeless. We have met few other people who are as sensitive to others' pain and as bold in moving into that pain as Dagny. Her testimony reminds us of the Apostle Paul's unreserved giving of himself in Christian service to others. He described himself as an "ambassador for Christ" in a ministry of reconciliation. He helped those in bondage to sin. He brought God's love to those estranged from him. He brought healing and wholeness (2 Cor 5:13-21). This is the mission that every believer is called to. What anchors such ministry? What drives people back into the dark caves to rescue? Paul's answer is profoundly straightforward: "Christ's love compels us" (2 Cor 5:14). We believe Paul is referring here both to love from Christ and the resultant love for Christ. Because Paul had experienced God's life-transforming love through Christ, he was overcome with the drive to share that love with others in need.

Many people mentored Dagny, helping her find healing and wholeness. Now she is supporting others to find their healing in Christ. She charges the darkness to rescue others, over and over again. One mentor (survivor) walking alongside another, and then another, and another, and another, and another—steadfast, genuine, honest, passionate, loving, committed, and faithful. These are the innate attributes of survivors who have been helped to heal. These are the attributes of the most effective mentors, God's unstoppable force.

Implications for Mentors:
Three Commitments

1. We Will Recruit in Order to Restore the Victimized

Recruit: (ri'kru:t) vb. To raise or strengthen by enlistment; to recover health or spirits; to furnish or be furnished with a fresh supply.

Rachel Lloyd, founder of GEMS (Girls Educational and Mentoring Services), one of the most respected domestic outreaches to prostituted girls and young women, speaks vulnerably from her own experiences. She says, "In my world, pimps are not managers, protectors, or 'market facilitators,' as one research study euphemistically called them, but leeches sucking the souls from beautiful, bright girls, predators who scour the streets, the group homes, and junior high schools stalking their prey."[151] Once a pimp gets inside a girl's head, he can begin to exploit her specific weaknesses, break down her defenses, and systematically groom her for selling her body. He may take pictures of her having sex for later blackmail, buy her nice clothes and then tell her that she must work off her "debt," convince her to "take care of him" and his needs, give her drugs in order to create an addiction, threaten her family, use her sexually, call her degrading names, heighten her false guilt and sexual shame, and use force, violence, or the threat of violence.

Therefore, as mentors, we strive to be better than a pimp at "recruiting" the girls back through love and faithful commitments of support and care. We must demonstrate a steadfast love for the girls that exhibits unilateral acts of love, expecting nothing in return. A pimp's intention is to get inside a girl's head by manipulation—to sadistically destroy and consume her. The mentor's intention is to show love so visible and real that the girl eventually begins to believe in the reality of being loved by a person who has *only* unselfish intentions of love. This happens as she experiences, over and over again, sacrificial gifts of love that are given to her, while taking nothing from her.

The sensitive mentor will build the survivor up, valuing and protecting her heart and body. The mentor will protect her by not exploiting her story and by providing for her basic needs, telling her that once she is well and strong she can "pay it forward" by doing the same for another exploited girl. We must lovingly and non-judgmentally care for the girl, while she recovers from the many effects of her abuse, including addiction. We might also be called to support and care for her non-offending family members and friends. We must protect her relationally and sexually, giving her new names such as "Princess" and "Daughter of a King" to lift her toxic shame. Through our consistent love, respect, and value, God will continue to heal her sexual shame. In short, we must offer the kind of divine love (agape) described in Scripture:

> *Love is patient. Love is kind. It does not envy,*
> *it does not boast, it is not proud.*
> *It is not rude, it is not self-seeking, it is not easily*
> *angered, it keeps no record of wrongs.*
> *Love does not delight in evil but rejoices*
> *with the truth.*
> *It always protects, always trusts, always hopes,*
> *always perseveres.*
> *Love never fails.*
> 1 CORINTHIANS 13:4–8

2. We Will Break the Bonds of Oppression and Its Debilitating Effects

> *Break: (breik) vb. To damage as to become inoperative; to crack with separating; to burst or cut the surface; to disperse; to fracture; to be weakened in spirit; to cause a person to give up; to reduce to poverty; to ruin.*

Most pimps and traffickers break a girl by establishing complete control. As mentioned earlier, the pimp manages and handles a girl by dictating what she wears, when and where she sleeps, what, when, and how much she eats, and how much air and light she is allowed to have. He socially isolates her, tortures her, exhausts her, sexually abuses her, and threatens her and her family. The successful pimp knows "everything about his ho," so that he can best break her down into total submission. He studies her insecurities so he can use them against her.

Therefore, as effective mentors, we will attempt to break a pimp's control over young victims by giving control and opportunity for self-mastery back to the girl. We support and nurture her by offering her choices such as: the clothes she wears, the food she eats, and the light that she is most comfortable with. We intentionally enlarge the girl's social support and stimulate her senses through music, dance, soothing aromas, and comforting words. Calm her. Help her to sleep. Support her family and friends. Posture humbly. Respect her. Affirm her. Support her through pregnancy when necessary, and help with the decisions she must make concerning her baby. Provide nutritious food, vitamins, medical care, and psychotropic medication (drugs used to treat depression/anxiety and other trauma effects on the brain and body) as needed. Help her define the rules that will make her and others feel safe in her home. Encourage her self-efficacy and empowerment. Be aware of her insecurities so that we can offer the highest level of sensitivity where she is most vulnerable—helping her validate and advocate for her previously unmet relational needs.

And we know that all things God works
for the good of those who love him, who have
been called according to his purposes.
If God is for us, who can be against us?
He who did not spare his own Son,
but gave him up for us all—
how will he not also,
along with him, graciously give us all things?
Who will bring any charge against those
whom God has chosen?
It is God who justifies. Who is he that
condemns?
Christ Jesus, who died—more than that,
who was raised to life—is at the right hand
of God and is also interceding for us.
Who shall separate us from the love of Christ?
Shall trouble or hardship or persecution
or famine or nakedness or danger or sword?
No, in all these things we are more than
conquerors through him who loved us.
For I am convinced that neither death nor life,
neither angels nor demons, neither the present
nor the future, nor any powers, neither height
nor depth, nor anything else in all creation,

will be able to separate us from the love of God
that is in Christ Jesus our Lord.
ROMANS 8:28, 31–35, 37–39

3. We Will Maintain Safe and Nurturing Relationships with the Girls for Their Ultimate Healing

Maintain: (meintein') vb. To continue or retain; keep in existence; to keep in proper or good condition; to enable a person to support a style of living; to defend against contradictions; uphold.

Most traffickers and organized gangs maintain control through establishing total financial dependency and debt, emotional dependency, and drug addiction. In time, they completely annihilate a girl's healthy self-identity. The pimp convinces the girl that he has total power over her. He pompously postures himself as the "ambassador of heaven and hell." He publicly humiliates her in order to destroy her self-worth, then postures manipulatively as the one who benevolently builds her back up. He repeats this cycle of abuse/comfort over and over again in an attempt to permanently bond the girl to himself. He isolates her by pulling her away from that which she loves and those who love her. He does whatever he can, wherever he can, to kill her spirit and to establish his total control over her body, mind, and soul.

Therefore, as emotionally healthy mentors we must maintain an environment of safety and consistent relational connection for our survivors' security and eventual healing. We will foster a relationship of interdependence, respecting each survivor's feelings, thoughts, and opinions.

We will demonstrate unselfish humility as "ambassadors of love," sent by an omnipotent and merciful Papa King who loves the survivor more than she can possibly know. Work to publicly affirm and praise the girl in order to build up her sense of self-value and worth. Encourage and validate God's original, unique design of her—her strengths and one-of-a-kind attributes. Affirm her over and over and over again, until she eventually becomes convinced of her true worth. We will listen and carry the pain of our survivor, and then comfort her in ways specific to her personality and needs.

This healing cycle, where the survivor expresses pain and subsequently receives comfort, is repeated over and over again in order to move the survivor through her grief and into vistas of life. We will walk with our survivor as she journeys through these cycles of pain and comfort for months and years to come.

As effective mentors, we will do whatever we can to bring the girl's spirit to life. We will wrap her in a network of long-term loving relationships. We will live out the love of God in such a way that the girl can, in time, begin to believe in a loving Papa King who created her with attributes of himself, a loving Papa King who sacrificed his only Son for her and stayed present with her throughout her abuse. Therefore, as she surrenders to her Papa King's love, he can and will redeem all of the evil that she has experienced, supernaturally transforming it into a victorious, empowered, and joy-filled life. One day her true Father and Papa King will call her into his literal kingdom—a place where there is no pain or loneliness or abuse; just the powerful love of her perfect Papa King.

The following Scripture passage is a love poem from God
to his daughters:

Therefore I am now going to allure her;
I will lead her into the desert and
speak tenderly to her.
There I will give her back her vineyards,
and will make the Valley of Achor [trouble]
a door of hope. There she will sing as in
the days of her youth,
as in the days she came up out
of Egypt [bondage].
I will betroth you to me forever;
I will betroth you in righteousness and
justice, in love and compassion.
I will betroth you in faithfulness,
and you will acknowledge the Lord.
HOSEA 2:14-15, 19-20

INTERACTIVE EXERCISE FOR THE GIRLS: SPARKLES

After reading aloud chapter twelve in *Princess Lost*, encourage honest sharing and discussion. Ask questions that encourage your survivor to connect with *her* feelings, thoughts,
and opinions. Remain validating and non-judging in your
responses in order to encourage free emotional expression.
If your survivor remains silent, encourage her by saying, "I
want you to know that it's okay for you to not talk right now.
You matter to me, and your feelings and thoughts are important. You are not alone in what you are experiencing—

I am here when you are ready to share. You will know when you are ready."

Provide clay. As your survivor listens to the music of *Princess Lost*, encourage her to close her eyes and to slowly manipulate the clay. Have her visualize herself running through the fields like the princess did in the story, with sparkles flying off her hands and feet. As she is able to do this, have her shape the clay into whatever shape she desires—a shape that reminds her of her own brilliance and sparkle. When she is finished, she can open her eyes and share what she has created. Dry the clay in the sun until it is hard so that she can keep it and paint it if she desires.

Some of the girls will also want to create music and dance that symbolize the sparkles that God has placed inside them—their unique brilliance as his image bearers.

∾
Appendix A:
Mentoring Safely[152]

1. **Know your limits.** Mentors guide and facilitate the self-discovery and connecting process of another. Mentors are not counselors, and they don't analyze, diagnose, or direct others. When it is possible, it is best for mentors to work under the supervision and direction of a professional mental health provider. Mentors facilitate and support the recovery process. Mentors are in the "real-life" community of the girl and are there when professionals cannot be. Ideally, the mentor relationship will be sustained long after the professional caregiver relationship is over.

2. **Don't take personally the behavior and responses of others.** Sarah's mentoring example below illustrates what it looks like to not personalize your survivor's struggles as rejection of you personally.

> In the beginning of our time together, Grace would become constantly overwhelmed with life. As a result, she would not respond to a phone call for days, and at other times would decline getting together for months. One day I asked her if she felt my invitations to spend time together were too overwhelming. She

told me she loved our meetings and to please keep calling. As our relationship progressed, she began to disclose to me the difficulties she was having with sleeping, nightmares, short-term memory loss, and boundaries. It became increasingly clear that her responses to these body/mind symptoms had no reflection on me as a mentor or a person. In the years before my healing, I had no boundaries and felt responsible for everything that was happening to me. I would have taken Grace's behavior as personal rejection and would have been thrown into a whirlwind of low self-esteem, possibly *reacting* to her instead of *responding* to her contingent upon her needs at the time.

3. **Don't answer for another person or interrupt.** Recognize your pull to emotionally rescue or control another.

4. **Don't overshare about your life.** Know the difference between appropriately "breaking the silence" by telling your own story and inappropriately dominating with your personal feelings and experiences.

5. **Resist the urge to defend your behavior.** If something you said felt offensive or hurtful to your survivor, just apologize. Instead of defending yourself, ask questions about what you can do differently next time that will feel more helpful.

6. **Give others the freedom to have their own set of conflicting feelings and experiences.** You must know where you end and the other person begins.

7. **Don't assume you can read another's thoughts.** You are not responsible to meet the needs of others if they have not articulated their feelings and needs.

8. **Don't accept the authority of others unquestioningly.** For instance, don't uncritically accept a pastor or other spiritual authority's words as the final say, particularly if they don't feel right. Continue to pray and search the Scriptures, asking God for discernment.

9. **Don't expect others to anticipate your needs.** Prayerfully reflect on your own needs and then articulate them to God as well as to others in your support community.

10. **Maintain sensitivity to boundary violations.** This includes your own boundaries, as well as the boundaries of others.

11. **Give respect, model respect, require respect.**

12. **Maintain your own relational support and accountability.**

13. **Practice soulcare and selfcare.**

Appendix B:
Mentoring Readiness

I am ready to be a mentor when I am emotionally freed to make the girls I mentor my focus. If I have not looked honestly at my own past to understand how the effects of sin have impacted me—both my own sinful patterns and others' sin perpetrated against me—then I will be hindered in guiding others through restoration. When I have done this work for myself, I will understand the role of pain in my life. This will create a humble and respectful posture as I engage in a mentoring relationship with others who have been wounded through abuse and exploitation.

I am ready to be a mentor when I have *developed the skills of moving into painful places and staying there while the Lord does his work on my heart.* Second Corinthians 1:3–7 will be my reality, as I will have learned how to experience God's comfort in my deepest pain, as opposed to relying on old patterns of denial and addiction to escape my own pain. I will be less likely to pull back from pain (mine or another's) because of this transformation in my life. I will have a story to share!

I will understand redemption personally, which will give me a passion for people and grace for the wounded. This understanding of pain will guide me as I offer comfort to others. I will not try to "rescue" others, but instead will sit in the mess, tolerating discomfort rather than trying to fix others.

I will have "magic eyes" to see what survivors cannot see in the midst of their pain. I will see and, at times, believe without seeing that God is actively at work redeeming their brokenness for his glory. This will produce patience and hope as I mentor others. I will know God has a plan for the healing of each individual he brings to himself.

I will remember that it is not my work, but the supernatural power of God's intervention upon a heart. Healing takes time, and I will join God as a participant in this supernatural process. I will manage my time appropriately, maintaining an emphasis on my own emotional and spiritual growth.

I will know and practice healthy boundaries as I mentor a survivor who has diminished or inappropriate boundaries. I will create safe space around her and freedom, so she can explore and define who it is that she wants to be. She will need my patience as she practices her voice—expressing feelings and needs, and setting her own boundaries.

I will maintain strong internal boundaries. I need to take myself safely to her level and help reconstruct her story without losing my sense of connection—to feel her story and to allow it to shape me without consuming me.

I will practice going to Jesus as my source of power, comfort, and strength. I will maintain my own supportive relationships so that I am freed to give to the one whom I am mentoring and not need *from* her. My emotional, relational, and spiritual needs must be met apart from my mentoring relationship.

Appendix C:
Self-Screen Questionnaire for Mentors

1. Have I sought help to heal from my own abuse or pain?
It is necessary to have experienced our own healing in order to be equipped and stable while guiding others through their healing. We cannot help another feel pain if we have not felt our own. The well of comfort we draw from as a mentor is the well of comfort we have received from God and others.

2. Have I worked hard on my personal recovery?
The process of healing is painful and requires rigorous honesty, vulnerability, and humility. It is a difficult journey, but a necessary one if we desire to be used as a mentor to others.

3. Have I identified my losses and grieved them?
Abuse robs us of many things that must be identified and felt. We cannot mentor another with something we have not done ourselves.

4. Have I identified my own sinful responses and repented?
Hurt people hurt people. Part of the healing process is asking God to reveal our own hurtful responses to the pain inflicted upon us, and to turn from those wrong responses. In recovery, we learn new and healthy ways to respond to our pain, with Jesus as our example. As mentors, we model and demonstrate healthy responses to painful events. We inspire others to choose healthy ways of dealing with pain and conflict. A sinless life is impossible to attain and, thankfully, not a requirement for mentoring. Honesty about our own destructive patterns creates a realness and authenticity in the caring relationship and protects it from self-righteousness.

5. Can I talk comfortably about my weaknesses?
We can only help others to the extent that we are willing to share our own shameful behaviors and pain in an open and vulnerable way. If we are not willing to share the painful and less-attractive parts of our story, God is not glorified—we are. We will only help others experience freedom from shame as we show how God is freeing us.

6. Am I struggling with an alcohol or drug problem? Am I struggling with other addictive behaviors?
Compulsive and addictive behaviors are fed by underlying pain. This pain must be faced in order to experience healing. Compulsions and addictions keep us from being fully present for others. Because mentoring can be emotionally intense and painful at times, we must have healthy strategies in place for dealing with our own pain. Mentors are to model healthy choices for others. This requires absolute sobriety.

7. **Am I currently in an abusive relationship?**
The book *Mending the Soul: Understanding and Healing Abuse* explains how abuse destroys. If you are in an abusive relationship, you are not in a place where you can focus properly on others. Christ desires your safety and healing first, before you try to offer help to others.

8. **Am I currently in a life crisis?**
Mentoring requires energy, stamina, and time. It is critically important that you evaluate your reserves and resources before promising to mentor others. Sexually exploited girls have been devastated by broken promises and relationships. It is imperative to evaluate yourself carefully so that you can **deliver more than you promise**.

9. **Do I desire to help others in order to feel good?**
Helping others heal feels good—especially when we see lives transformed and positively changed. However, if we need to experience "success" in order to feel good about ourselves, then we are not ready to mentor. There will be times when we will feel discouraged and extremely ineffective in this role. If our motivation is to feel good, we will burn out quickly.

10. **Am I interested in helping others to make amends for my past?**
If you are experiencing guilt over past choices and your desire to mentor is to make amends for your own shameful history, you will be ineffective and possibly harmful as a mentor. God's desire for you is to make amends for your past directly with the ones you have wronged. Only after you have done that will you be freed to focus on the girls whom you are seeking to love.

11. **Do I have a strong support network?**

Mentoring traumatized girls will require much of your heart. At times you will become discouraged, feel ineffective, carry intense anger, and feel extremely sad. You will need breaks and a solid selfcare protocol in order to sustain the compassion fatigue that is endemic to this ministry. It is best to build a solid network of loving and wise people to support you before beginning a mentoring relationship.

12. **Do I have a humble, teachable spirit?**

Walking alongside another in a healing relationship is the most sacred role we can take in another's life. It is imperative that we have a healthy sense of our unworthiness for this process and have embraced humbly our shortcomings. The safest relationship we can offer is one in which we come up underneath another, helping that person heal. We must demonstrate a positive respect for the personhood of others, no matter where they are or what they have done. We must see them as God sees them: made absolutely unique in his image. If we do not have this sense of awe in the presence of the survivor, it is best to not establish the relationship in the first place. They will know what you think of them, no matter how much you think you have hidden it. God is the one to give you his "eyes" of love.

13. **Do I have sufficient time to devote to a ministry of this kind?**

A mentoring relationship takes time. You will be called at various times of the day and night and will be asked to assist with all sorts of things that will probably cause discomfort. Take careful inventory of the time you have to give as a mentor, and share this at the beginning of the relationship. It will be helpful to discuss the nature of your relationship and the type and amount of support you are prepared to give. This will facilitate clearer boundaries and expectations at the onset of the relationship so that safety *and trust can be established. Remember, it is important to overdeliver rather than promise more than you can actually follow through with consistently.*

꩜

Appendix D:
Feeling Charts

Chart of Emotions

Mad	Sad	Glad	Afraid
Bothered	Down	At Ease	Uneasy
Ruffled	Blue	Comfortable	Apprehensive
Irritated	Somber	Relaxed	Careful
Displeased	Low	Contented	Cautious
Annoyed	Hurt	Optimistic	Hesitant
Steamed	Disappointed	Satisfied	Tense
Irked	Worn Out	Refreshed	Anxious
Perturbed	Melancholy	Grateful	Nervous
Frustrated	Downhearted	Pleased	Edgy
Angry	Unhappy	Warm	Distressed
Fed Up	Dissatisfied	Happy	Scared
Disgusted	Gloomy	Encouraged	Frightened
Indignant	Mournful	Tickled	Vulnerable
Resentful	Grieved	Proud	Repulsed
Ticked Off	Depressed	Hopeful	Agitated
Jealous	Lousy	Cheerful	Shocked
Fuming	Crushed	Thrilled	Alarmed
Explosive	Miserable	Delighted	Overwhelmed
Enraged	Defeated	Joyful	Frantic
Irate	Dejected	Elated	Panic Stricken
Incensed	Empty	Exhilarated	Horrified
Burned	Wretched	Overjoyed	Petrified
Outraged	Despairing	Ecstatic	Terrified
Furious	Devastated		Numb

Confused	Ashamed	Lonely
Curious	Uncomfortable	Out of Place
Uncertain	Awkward	Left Out
Ambivalent	Clumsy	Lonesome
Doubtful	Self-Conscious	Disconnected
Unsettled	Disconcerted	Insecure
Hesitant	Chagrined	Unappreciated
Perplexed	Abashed	Invisible
Puzzled	Embarrassed	Unwelcome
Muddled	Flustered	Misunderstood
Distracted	Sorry	Excluded
Flustered	Apologetic	Insignificant
Jumbled	Ashamed	Ignored
Unfocused	Regretful	Neglected
Fragmented	Remorseful	Removed
Dismayed	Guilty	Detached
Insecure	Disgusted	Isolated
Dazed	Belittled	Unwanted
Bewildered	Humiliated	Rejected
Lost	Violated	Deserted
Stunned	Dirty	Outcast
Chaotic	Mortified	Abandoned
Torn	Defiled	Withdrawn
Baffled	Devastated	Desolate
Dumbfounded	Degraded	Forsaken

Identify your emotions...
how do you feel?

Afraid	Angry	Anxious	Ashamed	Cheerful	Confused	Curious
Depressed	Disappointed	Disgusted	Embarrassed	Encouraged	Enraged	Glad
Gloomy	Grateful	Guilty	Hopeful	Hurt	Insecure	Insignificant
Invisible	Isolated	Jealous	Joyful	Lonely	Miserable	Misunderstood
Nervous	Overwhelmed	Proud	Puzzled	Regretful	Rejected	Resentful
Sad	Shocked	Unappreciated	Unsettled	Violated	Vulnerable	Withdrawn

∾
Endnotes

Foreward

1. Judith Herman, MD, *Trauma and Recovery: The Aftermath of Violence—from Domestic Abuse to Political Terror* (New York: Basic-Books, 1997), 38.
2. I have been impacted and shaped by the works of storytellers like George MacDonald, Calvin Miller, C. S. Lewis, and Frederick Buechner, and want to express my gratitude to them. In many ways, they have been my counselors and pastors, providing pathways for my heart.
3. C.S. Lewis, *Of Other Worlds: Essays and Stories,* (New York: Harcourt, 1966), 26.
4. This curriculum is created out of the research on sexually exploited girls and, therefore, it is designed for the caregivers of exploited girls (or survivors), since they make up most of this sexually exploited population. However, much of this material can be utilized and adapted in the treatment of male survivors.

Introduction

5. http://africa-love.livejournal.com.
6. Abby Tracy Live Journal, May 8, 2010; available at http://africa-love. livejournal.com.
7. Jay Albanese, *Commercial Sexual Exploitation of Children: What Do We Know and What Do We Do About It?* Washington, DC: U.S. Department of Justice, Office of Justice Programs, 2007; available at: https://www.ncjrs.gov/pdffiles1/nij/215733.pdf.
8. Available at: http://frwebgate.access.gpo.gov/cgi-bin/getdoc. cgi?dbname=106_cong_public_laws&docid=f:publ386.106;accessed 6/6/2011. This is similar in many respects to the United Nations, "Protocol to Prevent, Suppress and Punish Trafficking in Persons." On the latter, including the distinction between commercial sex trafficking and sexual abuse, see *Questions & Answers about the*

Commercial Sexual Exploitation of Children, 4th ed. (Bangkok, Thailand: ECPAT International, 2008); available at: www.ecpat.net.

9. Linda Smith, Samantha Healy Vardaman, and Melissa A. Snow, *The National Report on Domestic Sex Trafficking: America's Prostituted Children* (Vancouver, WA: Shared Hope International, 2009), 5.

10. Steven R. Tracy, *Mending the Soul: Understanding and Healing Abuse* (Grand Rapids: Zondervan, 2005), 27.

11. Modified from Toronto Crisis Center, "Rape," in *No Safe Place: Violence against Women and Children* (ed. Connie Guberman and Margie Wolfe; Toronto, Canada: Woman's Press, 1985), 62.

12. Ronald Barclay Allen, *The Majesty of Man: The Dignity of Being Human,* rev. ed. (Grand Rapids: Kregel, 2000), 45.

13. English Bible translations of Ps 8:5 vary, asserting that God made humans a little lower than: "God" (NASV; RSV; NRSV), "angels" (KJV; NKJV), or "heavenly beings" (NIV; ESV). The vast majority of Old Testament commentators agree that the Hebrew word used here (*eloheim*) is best translated "God." It is used over and over in Hebrew Scriptures this way. In a few rare instances *eloheim* is used of human rulers or of angels but indicates "God" unless the context dictates otherwise. In the Old Testament, angels are called "sons of God" but are almost never called *eloheim.*

14. C. S. Lewis, *The Weight of Glory and Other Addresses,* rev. ed. (New York: Macmillan, 1980) 45.

15. James Carse, *The Silence of God: Meditations on Prayer,* (New York: Macmillan, 1985), 54.

16. Pamela J. Birrell and Jennifer J. Freyd, "Betrayal Trauma: Relational Models of Harm and Healing," *Journal of Trauma and Practice* 5 (2006), 54.

17. J. V. Jordan, "Relational Resilience," Stone Center Working Paper Series, No. 57. Wellesley, MA (available at: http://www.wellesley.edu/JBMTI/publications/workinprogress.html).

18. Celestia G. Tracy, *Mending the Soul Workbook,* 3rd Edition (Phoenix: Global Hope Resources, 2009), 7.

19. The philosophical "problem of pain" is a complex one, but several truths are clear from Scripture: God is not the source of evil; God is good; God lovingly and effectively uses pain to make us more like Christ; God entrusts pain to his children for their good and His glory, cf. Gen 50:20; Acts 5:40–41; Col 1:24–27; James 1:2–4;

1 Pet 1:6–9. See also Steven R. Tracy, "Theodicy, Eschatology, and the Open View of God," in *Looking into the Future: Evangelical Studies in Eschatology*, (ed. David W. Baker, Grand Rapids: Baker, 2001), 295–312.

Chapter 1

20. Steven R. Tracy, *Mending the Soul: Understanding and Healing Abuse* (Grand Rapids: Zondervan, 2005), 97.
21. Ibid., 98.
22. C. Gilligan, *The Birth of Pleasure* (New York: Knopf, 2002), 6.
23. J. Herman, *Trauma and Recovery* (New York: BasicBooks, 1997), 107.
24. Steven Tracy, *Mending the Soul* (Grand Rapids: Zondervan, 2005), 100.
25. Eileen L. Zurbriggen et al., *Report of the APA Task Force on the Sexualization of Girls* (Washington, DC: American Psychological Association, 2010).

Chapter 2

26. 2 Cor 4:3–4, 11:3; 1 Tim 4:1; cp. 2 Kings 22:22.
27. The Apostle Paul followed such a strategy in 1 Cor 5:4–5, where he instructs married couples to prioritize meeting each other's sexual needs and not go too long without sexual intimacy lest in their sexual vulnerability Satan is able to tempt them with much greater potency.
28. Phyllis Kilbourn and Marjorie McDermid editors, *Sexually Exploited Children: Working to Protect and Heal* (Monrovia: MARC Publications, 1998), 208.
29. Foster W. Cline, *Sexually Exploited Children: Working to Protect and Heal* (Monrovia: MARC Publications, 1998), 213.
30. David Ziegler, *Traumatic Experience and the Brain; A Handbook for Understanding and Treating Those Traumatized as Children* (Phoenix: Acacia Publishing, 2002), 84.
31. GenoPro is an online support that offers additional explanations and help as needed.

Chapter 3

32. A number of excellent resources for spiritual care are found in chapter seven of the FAAST *Hands that Heal Academic Edition*

curriculum ("Understanding the Spiritual Needs of Survivors"). Other helpful spiritual care resources are: *Helping Victims of Sexual Abuse: A Sensitive Biblical Guide for Counselors, Victims, and Families* by Lynn Heitritter and Jeanette Vought; *Sexually Exploited Children: Working to Protect and Heal,* edited by P. Kilbourn and M. McDermid (especially the chapter by D. Brewster "Spiritual Healing"); Steven Tracy, *Mending the Soul* (especially chapter five "Shame" and chapter eight "Rebuilding Intimacy with God").

33. Steven R. Tracy, "Rationalization for a Faith-Based Approach to the Problem of Prostituted Adolescent Girls," (2009).

34. On the way pornography and our pornified culture have distorted healthy sexuality, see Celestia G. and Steven R. Tracy, *Forever and Always: The Art of Intimacy* (Eugene, OR: Wipf & Stock, 2011), 31–40, 111–12, 139-40, 143.

35. We generally use the name "Hope" as the pseudonym for individual sexually trafficked girls. It conveys our posture toward them. In spite of all they have been through, based on our faith in God's powerful, redeeming love, we believe they have hope.

Chapter 4

36. Lam 1:3, 4, 7; 16; 2:15; 3:4, 17; 5:8–16; cited from S. Tracy, *Mending the Soul,* 155.

37. For a discussion of loss and grief experienced by sex-trafficking survivors and practical exercises for healing, see Elizabeth Peffer Talbot et al., "Understanding the Psychological Needs of Survivors," *Hands that Heal: International Curriculum to Train Trafficking Survivors,* Academic Edition, 183-94.

38. Intrusive symptoms include re-experiencing traumatic events, often through nightmares, daydreams, thoughts, or triggering images. Intrusive symptoms can also be a feeling of distress or anxiety when reminded, by a trigger or in discussion, of the traumatic event.

39. Healing art is available on the Mending the Soul Ministries website: www.mendingthesoul.org.

40. J. Myers et al., *The APSAC Handbook on Child Maltreatment, 2nd Edition* (London: Sage Publications, 2002), 145.

41. For a more detailed discussion of how abuse survivors can "reimage the Fatherhood of God," see Steven Tracy, *Mending the Soul,*

166–71. Portions of this section are drawn from this section of *Mending the Soul.*

42. John Cooper, *Our Father in Heaven: Christian Faith and Inclusive Language for God* (Grand Rapids: Baker, 1998), 261.

43. List taken from Steven Tracy, *Mending the Soul,* 168.

44. Repeatedly in Revelation we find that divine judgment is coming because of evil human and demonic powers who killed, tormented, and otherwise abused the innocent, cf. Rev 6:9–11; 11:7; 12:13–14; 17:6; 18:24. In Rev 18:11–14 we see judgment on wicked merchants who traded in various goods, including "the bodies and souls of men" (v. 14). In ancient Rome, while slavery was legal, slave traders were considered to be particularly immoral and lawless (cf. 1 Tim 1:10). For an excellent discussion of the vices of ancient slave traders, including sexual abuse and prostitution, see J. Albert Harrill, *Slaves in the New Testament: Literary, Social, and Moral Dimensions* (Minneapolis: Fortress, 2006), 119–144.

45. Judith Herman, *Trauma and Recovery: The Aftermath of Violence— From Domestic Abuse to Political Terror* (New York: BasicBooks, 1997), 140.

46. I. L. McCann and L. A. Pearlman, "Vicarious Traumatization: A Framework for Understanding the Psychological Effects of Working with Victims," *Journal of Traumatic Stress* 3 (1990): 131–50.

47. Clawson & Grace, *Finding a Path to Recovery.*

Chapter 5

48. Stoltz, J. M. et al., "Associations between childhood maltreatment and sex work in a cohort of drug-using youth," *Social Science and Medicine* 65 (2007): 1214-21.

49. M. H. Silbert & A. M. Pines, "Early sexual exploitation as an influence in prostitution," *Social Work* (1983): 285-89; cf. also C. S. Widom & J.B. Kuhns, "Childhood victimization and subsequent risk for promiscuity, prostitution, and teenage pregnancy: A prospective study," *American Journal of Public Health,* 86 (1996): 1607-12.

50. K. A. Tyler et al., "The impact of childhood sexual abuse on later sexual victimization among runaway youth," *Journal of Research on Adolescence,* 11 (2001): 151–76.

51. Ian Urbana, "For Runaways, Sex Buys Survival," *The New York Times,* October 27, 2009.

52. R. F. Anda, et al., "The Enduring Effects of Abuse and Related Adverse Experiences in Childhood," *European Archives of Psychiatry and Clinical Neuroscience* 256 (2006): 174–186.
53. Cathy S. Widom and Michael G. Maxfield, "An Update on the Cycle of Violence," *Research in Brief,* Washington, DC: U.S. Department of Justice, National Institute of Justice, 2001.
54. For further discussion of the concept of sexuality being a divine gift designed to lead to intimate relationships ultimately patterned after God himself, see Celestia and Steven Tracy, *Forever and Always,* 3–21, 47–59.
55. Matt 3:16–17, 28:18–19, John 3:35–36, 10:30, 14:10–11, 16:32, 17:5, 21.
56. Prov 5:15–20; Song of Sol 7:1–13; Heb 13:4.
57. Lev 20:10–13; Deut 22:20–21, 1 Cor 5:9–11; 6:9.
58. See Steven Tracy, *Mending the Soul* (Grand Rapids: Zondervan, 2005), 73–91.
59. Ibid., 112–117.
60. Jeannie G. Noll, Penelope K. Trickett, and Frank Putnam, "A Prospective Investigation of the Impact of Childhood Sexual Abuse on the Development of Sexuality," *Journal of Consulting and Clinical Psychology* 71 (2003): 575–86; Jacob M. Vigil, David C. Geary, Jennifer Byrd-Craven, "A Life History Assessment of Early Childhood Sexual Abuse in Women," *Developmental Psychology* 41 (2005): 553–61.
61. William N. Friedrich, Patricia Grambsch, Linda Damon, "Child Sexual Behavior Inventory: Normative and Clinical Comparisons," *Psychological Assessment* 4 (1992): 303–11.
62. Mary Jane Rotheram-Borus, Karen A. Mahler, and Cheryl Koopman, "Sexual Abuse History and Associated Multiple Risk Behavior in Adolescent Runaways," *American Journal of Orthopsychiatry* 66 (1996): 390–400; Theresa E. Senn, Michael P. Carey, and Peter A. Vanable, "Childhood Sexual Abuse and Sexual Risk Behavior among Men and Women Attending a Sexually Transmitted Disease Clinic," *Journal of Consulting and Clinical Psychology* 74 (2006): 720–31.
63. M. D. De Bellis et al., "Hypothalmic-Pituitary-Adrenal Axis Dysregulation in Sexually Abused Girls," *Journal of Clinical Endocrinology and Metabolism* 78 (1994): 249–255; Mark G. Haviland, et al., "Thyroid Hormone Levels and Psychological Symptoms

in Sexually Abused Adolescent Girls," *Child Abuse & Neglect* 30 (2006): 589–98.

64. A. Browne and D. Finkelhor, "Impact of Child Sexual Abuse: A Review of the Research," *Psychological Bulletin* 99 (1985): 152.

65. C. M. Arata, "Child Sexual Abuse and Sexual Revictimization," *Clinical Psychology: Science and Practice* 9 (2002): 135–164; Catherine C. Classen, Oxana Gronskaya Palesh, and Rashi Aggarwal, "Sexual Revictimization: A Review of the Empirical Literature," *Trauma, Violence & Abuse* 6 (2005): 103–129; A. A. Roodman and A. A. Clum, "Victimization Rates and Method Variance: A Meta-Analysis," *Journal of Traumatic Stress* 21 (2001): 183–204.

66. Classen, Palesh, and Aggarwal, "Sexual Revictimization: A Review of the Empirical Literature." See also J. Coid, et al., "Relation between Childhood Sexual and Physical Abuse and Risk of Revictimisation in Women: A Cross-Sectional Survey," *Lancet* 358 (2001): 450–54.

67. David Finkelhor, Richard K. Ormrod, and Heather A. Turner, "Re-victimization Patterns in a National Longitudinal Sample of Children and Youth," *Child Abuse & Neglect* 31 (2007): 479–502.

68. Bonnie L. Kessler and Kathleen J. Bieschke, "Retrospective Analysis of Shame, Dissociation, and Adult Victimization in Survivors of Childhood Sexual Abuse," *Journal of Counseling Psychology* 46 (1999): 335–341.

69. R. P. Kluft, "Dissociation and Subsequent Vulnerability: A Preliminary Study," *Dissociation* 3 (1990): 167–73.

70. Jennifer L. Steel and Claes A. Herlitz, "The Association between Childhood and Adolescent Sexual Abuse and Proxies for Sexual Risk Behavior," *Child Abuse & Neglect* 29 (2005): 1141–1153.

71. Brian P. Marx, Jennifer M Heidt, and Sari D. Gold, "Perceived Uncontrollability and Unpredictability, Self-Regulation, and Sexual Revictimization," *Review of General Psychology* 9 (2005): 67–90.

72. Ibid., 179.

73. P.A. Boudeyns, et al., "PTSD Among Vietnam Veterans: An Early Look at Treatment Outcome Using Direct Therapeutic Exposure," *Journal of Traumatic Stress* 3 (1990): 359–68.

Chapter 6

74. Ian Urbina, "Running in the Shadows: For Runaways, Sex Buys

Survival," *The New York Times*, October 27, 2009. Urbina attributed this quote to a pimp named Harvey Washington "who began serving a four-year sentence in Arizona in 2005 for pandering a 17-year-old and three adult prostitutes."
75. This reflects research on juvenile prostitution in North America.
76. Cusick, L., "Youth prostitution: A literature review," *Child Abuse Review* 11 (2002): 230–251; Hwang, S.-L. & O. Bedford, "Precursors and pathways to adolescent prostitution in Taiwan," *The Journal of Sex Research* 40 (2003): 201–210; L. M. Williams, & M. E. Frederick, *Pathways into and out of commercial sexual victimization of children: Understanding and responding to sexually exploited teens.* (Lowell, MA: University of Massachusetts Lowell, 2009).
77. In terms of education, the correlation is so strong that some researchers postulate that each additional school year completed lowers the risk of entering prostitution by 12 percent. This educational protective factor is not simply about the acquisition of knowledge and a diploma but reflects the positive social and emotional impact of regular school attendance.
78. Ross and Elizabeth Clarke, "Relating Current Research on Prostitution to the Needs of Sexually Exploited Youth: An Examination of Their Social and Psychological Histories and Implications for Treatment," Research paper, Arizona State University, 2010, 12.
79. Bessel A. van der Kolk, MD, *Psychological Trauma* (Washington, DC: American Psychiatric Press, 1987), 14–15.
80. J. Bowlby, *Separation: Anxiety and Anger* (New York: Basic Books, 1973).
81. Ibid., 78–80.
82. Ibid., 32.
83. J. Bowlby, "Violence in the Family as a Disorder of the Attachment and Caregiving Systems," *American Journal Psychoanalysis* 44 (1984): 9–27.
84. Bessel A. van der Kolk, *Psychological Trauma*, 15.
85. John Bowlby, *A Secure Base: Parent-Child Attachment and Healthy Human Development* (New York: Basic Books, 1988); see also Robert Karen, *Becoming Attached: First Relationships and How They Shape Our Capacity to Love* (New York: Oxford University Press, 1994).
86. W.A. Mason, "Motivational Aspects of Social Responsiveness in Young Chimpanzees," in Early Behavior: Comparative and

Developmental Aspects (ed. H. Stevenson; New York: John Wiley and Sons, 1967) cited by van der Kolk, *Psychologial Trauma*, 42-43.

Chapter 7

87. Diana E. Russell, "The Making of a Whore," *Violence Against Women* 1 (1995): 77–98.
88. Calvin Miller, Symphony Trilogy.
89. *The Illustrated Bible Dictionary*, vol. 3, s.v. "Shame" (Downers Grove: InterVarsity, 1980), 1427.
90. Lewis B. Smedes, *Shame and Grace: Healing the Shame We Don't Deserve* (New York: HarperCollins, 1993), 37.
91. Jesus's words are quite relevant here: "But if anyone causes one of these little ones who believe in me to sin, it would be better for him to have a large millstone hung around his neck and to be drowned in the depths of the sea. Woe to the world because of the things that cause people to sin! Such things must come, but woe to the man through whom they come!" (Matt 18:6–7). In other words, adults by their mistreatment of children can "cause" children to sin (and hence experience more shame). But woe to the adult who does this!
92. Candice Feiring, Lynn Taska, and Michael Lewis, "The Role of Shame and Attributional Style in Children's and Adolescents' Adaptation to Sexual Abuse," *Child Maltreatment* 3 (1998): 130.
93. Candice Feiring, Lynn Taska, and Michael Lewis, "Adjustment Following Sexual Abuse Discovery: The Role of Shame and Attributional Style," *Developmental Psychology* 38 (2002): 87.
94. J. Herman, *Trauma and Recovery*, 52–53.
95. H. B. Lewis, *Shame and Guilt in Neurosis* (New York: International University Press, 1971) as quoted by J. Herman, *Trauma and Recovery*, p.53.
96. Ibid., 53.
97. R. J. Lifton, "The Concept of the Survivor," in *Survivors, Victims, and Perpetrators: Essays on the Nazi Holocaust*; (ed. J. E. Dimsdale (New York: International Universities Press, 1971), 113–26.
98. John Money, Charles Annecillo, and June Werlwas Hutchison, "Forensic and Family Psychiatry in Abuse Dwarfism: Munchausen's Syndrome by Proxy, Atonement, and Addiction to Abuse," *Journal of Sex and Marital Therapy* 2, (1985): 35.

99. Patrick J. Carnes, PhD, *The Betrayal Bond; Breaking Free of Exploitive Relationships* (Deerfield Beach: Health Communications, 1997), 31–36.
100. Bessel van der Kolk, "The Trauma Spectrum: The Interaction of Biological and Social Events in the Genesis of the Trauma Response," *Journal of Traumatic Stress* 1, no. 3 (1988): 286. As quoted by P. Carnes, *The Betrayal Bond*, 33.
101. Bessel van der Kolk, *Psychological Trauma*, 73.
102. Ibid., 36.
103. David Ziegler, *Traumatic Experience and the Brain*, 158.

Chapter 8
104. Calvin Miller, *A Requiem for Love* (Dallas: Word Publishing, 1989), 128.
105. Melissa Farley, *Prostitution & Trafficking in Nevada: Making the Connections* (San Francisco: Prostitution Research and Education, 2007), 49–84.
106. Ibid. 51.
107. Robert D. Hare, "Psychopathy Checklist-Revised: (PCL-R) 2nd Edition." For more information see Robert Hare's website at: www.hare.org.
108. Mickey Royal, *The Pimp Game: Instructional Guide* (Los Angeles: Sharif Publishing, 1998). Royal's book and website indicates he is or has been a pimp.
109. Victor Malerek, *The Johns: Sex for Sale and the Men Who Buy It* (New York: Arcade Publishing, 2009), 81.
110. Ibid, 82–83.
111. Nixon, K. et al., "The Everyday Occurrence: Violence in the Lives of Girls Exploited through Prostitution," *Violence Against Women* 8 (2002): 1016.
112. Hilary L. Surratt, et al., "The Connections of Mental Health Problems, Violent Life Experiences, and the Social Milieu of the 'Stroll' with the HIV Risk Behaviors of Female Street Sex Workers," *Journal of Psychology & Human Sexuality 17* (2005): 33.
113. Melissa Farley, et al., "Prostitution and trafficking in nine countries: An update on violence and posttraumatic stress disorder," in M. Farley, ed., *Prostitution, trafficking, and traumatic stress* (Birmingham, NY: The Haworth Maltreatment & Trauma Press, 2003), 43, 55.

114. Dalla, R. L., Y. Xia, and Kennedy, H, "You just give them what they want and pray they don't kill you: street-level sex workers' reports of victimization, personal resources, and coping strategies," *Violence Against Women* 9 (2003): 1367–1394.
115. Rebecca Harvey, "A closer look at residential treatment programs for women exiting prostitution," Doctoral dissertation, Pepperdine University Graduate School of Education and Psychology, 2008.
116. Surratt et al., "The Connections of Mental Health Problems, Violent Life Experiences, and the Social Milieu of the 'Stroll.'
117. L. A. Kramer, "Emotional experiences of performing prostitution," in M. Farley, Ed., *Prostitution, trafficking, and traumatic stress* (Birmingham, NY: The Haworth Maltreatment & Trauma Press, 2003), 195.

Chapter 9
118. Donald Bloesch, *God the Almighty: Power, Wisdom, Holiness, Love* (Downers Grove, IL: InterVarsity, 1995), 151–52, 145, emphasis mine.
119. Randy Alcorn, *The Grace and Truth Paradox: Responding with Christlike Balance* (Sisters, OR: Multnomah Publishers, 2003), 35.
120. C. S. Lewis, *The Screwtape Letters and Screwtape Proposes a Toast* (New York: MacMillan, 1961), xi.
121. Ibid.
122. Matt 9:9–13, 36; 14:14, 15:32, 20:34; Luke 7:13; cp. Matt 18:27; Luke 10:33; 15:20.
123. Phyllis Kilbourn, "Compassionate Care for Caregivers," in *Sexually Exploited Children: Working to Protect and Heal* (ed. P. Kilbourn and M. McDermid; Monrovia, CA: MARK, 1998), 297.
124. Ibid. 303–6.
125. Abby Tracy Live Journal, October 2, 2007.
126. John 13:23, 20:2, 21:7, 20.
127. Abby Tracy Live Journal, September 29, 2008; available at: africa-love.livejournal.com.

Chapter 10
128. Gary Haugen, *Terrify No More: Young Girls Held Captive and the Daring Undercover Operations to Win Their Freedom* (Nashville: Thomas Nelson, 2005), 118.

129. Linda Smith, *Renting Lacy: A Story of America's Prostituted Children* (Vancouver, WA: Shared Hope International, 2009), 112.
130. Joel B. Green, The Theology of the Gospel of Luke (Cambridge: Cambridge University Press, 1995), 76. Green notes that the way Luke elsewhere uses the themes found in Luke 4:18 shows that this passage summarizes Jesus' mission. See, for instance, Luke 7:1–22 and Acts 10:38.
131. Luke 1:77, 7:42–43, 13:10–17, 24:47; Acts 8:22–23, 10:38, 13:38–39, 26:18.
132. Pss 2:1–5, 110:1–6; Matt 13:39; Acts 4:25–26; 2 Cor 4:4; Eph 2:2; Rev 12:7–12.
133. Gen 34:1–2, 31, 38:1–26; Lev 19:29; 2 Chron 21:11–15; Amos 7:17; John 8:3–11. It is indisputable that the vast majority of domestic and global prostitution reflects and is causally linked to poverty, injustice, abuse, and patriarchy. A few of the published works that demonstrate this are: B. Schissel and K. Fedec, "The selling of innocence: The gestalt of danger in the lives of youth prostitutes," *Canadian Journal of Criminology* (1999): 33–56; J. G. Silverman et al., "Experiences of sex trafficking victims in Mumbai, India," *International Journal of Gynecology and Obstetrics 97* (2007): 221–226; J. Raphael, *Listening to Olivia: Violence, Poverty and Prostitution*. (Lebanon, NH: Northeastern University Press, 2004).
134. Matt 23:1–36; Luke 7:36–50, 11:39–42; John 8:3–11; 9:13–34.
135. John Stott, *Human Rights and Human Wrongs: Major Issues for a New Century*, 3rd ed. (Grand Rapids: Baker, 1999), 39.
136. M. Farley, and H. Barkan, "Prostitution, violence, and post-traumatic stress disorder," *Women and Health 27* (1998): 37–49. S. L. Hwang and O. Bedford, "Juveniles' motivations for remaining in prostitution," *Psychology of Women Quarterly 28* (2004): 136–146. See also L. M. Williams and M. E. Frederick, "Pathways into and out of commercial sexual victimization of children: Understanding and responding to sexually exploited teens."

Chapter 11
137. S. L. Hwang & O. Bedford, "Juveniles' motivations for remaining in prostitution," *Psychology of Women Quarterly 28* (2004): 136–146. See also L. M. Williams & M. E. Frederick, "Pathways into and out

of commercial sexual victimization of children: Understanding and responding to sexually exploited teens."

138. Some of the best material we have seen for addressing the spiritual needs of the sexually exploited and prostituted is that of Beth Grant and Cindy Lopez, eds., *Hands that Heal International Curriculum to Train Caregivers of Trafficking Survivors: Academic Edition* (2007), 217–37.

139. Dawn Herzog Jewell, *Escaping the Devil's Bedroom* (Grand Rapids: Monarch Books, 2008), 87–8.

140. Ps 103:11–12; Rom 3:21–22, 4:3–5; Heb 7:24–27, 10:17–22.

141. 2 Cor 3:8; 1 Pet 2:2; 2 Pet 3:8.

142. Rom 8:30; Eph 5:27; Col 1:22.

143. 1 Cor 11:1; Phil 4:9; Heb 13:7.

144. Gary A. Haugen, *Just Courage: God's Great Expedition for the Restless Christian* (Downers Grove, IL: InterVarsity, 2008), 82.

145. Satan and: prostitution—Lev 17:7, 20:6; Nah 3:4; slavery and bondage—Is 14:3–4; Nah 3:4; Luke 4:33–35, 8:29, 9:38–42, 13:16, 2 Tim 2:26; abuse and destructive violence—Job 1:12–19; Matt 17:15–18; Luke 8:32–33; 22:3; John 8:44; Rev 2:10, 9:3–11, 12:13–17.

146. Satan as the: destroyer— Rev 9:11; deceiver—John 8:44; 2 Cor 11:3, 13–15; 1 Tim 2:14; Rev 12:9, 20:3; evil one—Matt 5:7, 6:13; John 17:15; 2 Thess 3:3; 1 John 2:13–14.

147. Gerry Breshears, "Basic Principles for Dealing with the Demonic," 2010.

148. Calvin Miller, *A Requiem for Love* (Dallas: Word Publishing, 1989), 90.

149. L. Cozolino, *The Making of a Therapist: A Practical Guide for the Inner Journey* (New York: W. W. Norton & Co, 2004), xv–xvi.

Chapter 12

150. Evangelicals, particularly those not in the Charismatic or Pentecostal traditions, are often uncomfortable with the idea of God speaking through dreams. Thus, a few comments are in order. (1) Our human experiences and impressions, including dreams, are fallible and must be interpreted through the lens of Scripture (Deut 13:1–5; Jer 23:25–32; 2 Pet 1:16–21). (2) The New Testament describes the Christian life as an intimate and dynamic spiritual experience in which the Spirit guides and relates to

believers in a personal (John 16:13; 1 Cor 2:10–13; Rom 8:13–16) and individual (Acts 16:6–7, 20:22; 1 Thess 5:18–21) manner. (3) Throughout biblical history we find God frequently speaking to people through dreams (Gen 31:10–13, 24; 37:5–7, 40:5–8; 41:1–8; Judg 7:13; 1 Kings 3:5; Dan 2:1–45; Matt 1:20, 2:12–13). (4) In the church age in which believers are indwelt by the Holy Spirit, God continues to speak to his children through dreams and visions (Acts 9:10, 12, 10:3, 9–16). In fact, this is identified as a characteristic of the "last days" in which we live (Acts 2:17; Joel 2:28).
151. Rachel Lloyd, *Girls Like Us: Fighting for a World Where Girls Are Not for Sale, an Activist Finds Her Calling and Heals Herself* (New York, NY: HarperCollins, 2011), 90.

Appendix
152. Sarah Parks helped to create this list as a result of her MTS mentoring and facilitating.

Subject Index

Scripture Index